Shouting at Leaves

Jennifer Msumba

Dedicated to my mom
Thank you for everything always
My protector
My first fan
My teacher
I love you the most-est.

And to my loyal and true people who
Set me free to be myself
And to live my best life.

Special thanks to: Jennie Ellis

CHAPTER 1

It All Makes Sense Now

"Mommy, today's gonna be a good day."

I walked with them down the hall slowly, as if I was walking to my death. *Dead Jen walking!* I thought to myself with some sort of dark humor, trying to keep the dread from taking over. My stomach was sick and my body was cold. I tried to muster up strength and bravery for whatever pain lay ahead.

We entered an empty classroom where there lay a four-point board in the middle. Nothing else. Even with the blinds wide open, sunlight refused to pour in, as if the day knew to be respectful of my impending doom. I didn't fight even though I knew something beyond terror was coming. I forced myself into a matter-of-fact calm. This was going to be bad. This was going to hurt—but I wasn't going to let them see my fear. I was not going to give them the satisfaction of knowing my terror. My life flashed before my eyes. How in the world did this become my reality?

* * * * *

Mom and I walked hand in hand across the parking lot into the mall. The year was 1979 and I was three years old. The local mall was a happy, thriving shopper's destination. But for me it was a nightmare. Not five minutes into our trip, the floor beneath me began to shift and contort like a funhouse mirror. The items on the shelves had blended together into a swirly, whirly, blurry, enveloping fog. I felt like I was attempting to walk on an uneven surface that kept changing and morphing into new twists and dips. I tried to compensate and find my balance, but I couldn't see through the fog in front of me. I clung to my mom's leg, terrified the floor would swallow me. I closed my eyes and waited desperately to get out of there.

"What is wrong, Jenny?" my mom asked as I tugged on her leg. But I did not have the words to answer her. Once we left the chaos and got into the open parking lot, the ground started to settle, and the air cleared. After around twenty minutes of riding in the car, I felt like myself again.

This was a regularly occurring episode for me.

In my mind I desperately wanted to tell my mom about the swirly, whirly colors and shape-shifting floor, but I didn't have the words. I was able to use words to express my needs and wants, but I had no words for my feelings. Especially ones as bizarre as these.

Looking back, it's clear to me that my little brain and young sensory system couldn't handle the busyness of the mall. The diverse-colored items lining the shelves, the sound of the blenders at Orange Julius, along with the mixed smells of pizza and gyros coming from the food court were too much. The swarm of people, each one coming with his or her own smell, sound, and color were simply staggering. My senses, in turn, short-circuited and couldn't process the information I needed. To this day I still get overwhelmed in busy places; as an adult, however, I am able to understand why it is happening so I can manage it.

I was a happy and positive child. My mom recalls that every morning when she would wake me I would declare, "Mommy, today's gonna be a good day." My optimistic spirit was there from the start. I would later fight to preserve this precious gift from God.

When I was three, my mom taught me to read simple books. I fell in *love* with words. I was insatiably eager to read and spell new words so I could keep up with my two older brothers. Words made sense because language came with a set of rules. If you followed these rules you could read and spell even *more* words! I loved rules and structure. They made me feel safe. In no time, I was trying to read everything I could get my hands on. I loved getting my brothers' church magazines and circling every word I knew. I wouldn't cheat. I painstakingly circled only the words I could read, every "the," "and," "but," and "God" I could find. Only words I knew—that was my rule.

This was just the beginning of the rules I would create for myself in an attempt to keep my world predictable.

During this same time, my older sister began attending the local high school. My mom and I would drop her off every morning. I looked forward to car rides. I loved to stare out the window, unfocus my eyes, and let the movement of the trees and houses relax my brain. The blur gave me a kind of high, as I would become super focused on a single point in the distance. I had a hard time looking away. I would go into another world and it was hard to bring myself back to the real one.

This was a stark—and welcome—contrast to my everyday experience with the chaotic world. One particular day, a street sign that we had passed many times suddenly came into focus. I could read it: "Not a Tough Street." What did it mean? Then it hit me and I shouted to my mom, "Mommy, that's not a tough street! We can go down that street!"

Being one to take things literally, "Not a tough street" meant to me that it was a safe street with no high school kids allowed. I was terrified of the high schoolers, who looked like thugs to me with their ripped jean jackets and cigarettes (this was the 1980s when students were allowed to smoke outside). I was so happy. The rules worked on Not-a-Tough-Street. My mom thought this was the cutest thing ever, but being a teacher and lover of words, she corrected me. She explained the sign actually read "Not a *Through* Street," which had a totally different meaning. She congratulated me on my close attempt, and that became a story we enjoy to this day. I found a way to tell my mom my feelings through a misreading of a sign. What a gift!

By age five I was able to articulate more specifically, However I started to hide my strange sensory experiences. For example, the feeling of meat in my mouth had at one point become unbearable. I don't know if it was the fatty feeling but I did not want to chew it nor swallow it. Instead of expressing that, I simply said, "I don't like it." That was all I could make sense of at the time. All my family knew was that one day I developed an aversion to meat. They couldn't understand it, but my dad loved to cook so he would make me a separate vegetarian option. Vegetables didn't have the repulsive texture of meat.

My favorite meal was Tender Tips. They were made of soy or whey protein and my dad would fry them up in a pan with seasoning. I loved Tender Tips! I couldn't pronounce them correctly and I called them Pretend-a-tips—which is kind of funny since they *were* pretend meat.

After dinner, my job as the youngest child was to empty the clean dishes out of the dishwasher. For most people, this would not be a daunting task, but for me the feeling of the squeaky-clean glasses and dishes on my hands was too intense. The sensation was like nails on a chalkboard or styrofoam rubbing together. The feeling would shoot up my body and make me shudder. I loathed this chore. I would try every tactic to get out of it. It wasn't that I was disobedient; it was that the sensations were too much.

I believed my mom would not understand that I found touching the dishes intolerable. Even at my young age, I had begun to realize that I was different. My family and friends did not seem affected by squeaky glasses, odd textures, and loud noises. Eventually I found a coping mechanism, which would become a common practice for me in life. To avoid that terrible feeling, I kept my hands wet while I was touching the dishes. Every three or four dishes I would have to re-wet my hands. This perplexed my mom. She would ask me why I kept doing this, but all I could muster was a shoulder shrug and an "I don't know." Why didn't I just tell her? Why didn't I believe she would understand?

I don't know.

According to my mom, I was a very happy and outgoing baby. However, around the age of two I suddenly stopped wanting to interact with people and preferred to play by myself. My understanding is that age two is when autism starts to be noticeable. But my family didn't know at the time that I would be diagnosed with autism.

I stopped letting people hold me, except my immediate family. I would scream and cry if anyone else tried to touch or interact with me. I remember hating it because it felt like I was being poked all over with a dull object. I felt suffocated and confined. The rough skin, the smells, the voices in my ears were terrifying and unpredictable. I just wanted my mom. She was soft and familiar and she spoke quietly in my ears.

My mom worried that I had developed an aversion to other people so she enrolled me in preschool. She thought maybe I simply needed to develop better social skills.

The start of a school year always means new shoes. I love new shoes! I remember specifically: she took me to get them at Thom McAn, a popular shoe store at the time. She was showing me all the cute little pink sneakers with bows on them, but it was too late. Something else had caught my eye. I spotted the most amazing pair of little brown construction boots and I knew they were mine. I grabbed my mom's hand and said, "Mommy…'struction boots!" But to my dismay, she was not as impressed as I was. She gently tried to lead me back to the little pink sneakers, but I just dug in more. "Mommy, 'struction boots!" That was it. I was fixated.

My mom, being the incredible person she is, made me a deal. She said we would come back to the store the next day, and if I still wanted the boots, I could have them. I thought about those boots all night. The next day, sure enough, I was walking out of the store with my new boots on and they felt great! I liked the structure of them. The pressure around my feet and ankles soothed me and calmed my body. I had preferred boys' clothes because they felt more comfortable to me and they never had itchy lace, bows, or sequins on them. They were soft, plain, sensible, and predictable.

Off to preschool I went. Only it didn't go quite that smoothly. When I realized my mom was going to leave, I lost it. I was so afraid because I did not want to be separated from her. She was my safe place. I remember crying and crying in the beginning. Eventually the teachers told me that if I kept it up, I would be put into the baby room because I was acting like a baby. This terrified me even more. Eventually I calmed down and settled into the routine. I remember enjoying recess because I loved to be outside. I also liked naptime, even though I wouldn't sleep, because it was quiet and dark and cool. Sweet relief for my senses. I remember struggling when nap time was over because of the transition from quiet back to all the activity. I dreaded it.

Dread would become a familiar feeling in my life. It would taunt me, it would be there to provoke me—just out of reach and out of my control.

CHAPTER 2

Jennifer–a Well-Loved Child

"Don't be scared, Love. You belong."

My name is Jennifer Msumba. I grew up in Andover, Massachusetts—a quiet, leafy suburb north of Boston. I am the youngest of four children. I have two older brothers and one older sister. My mom is Italian-American, and my dad is from Malawi, Africa. This is the story of my experience with autism. It ends up like the lyrics of a song a wrote:

> *5 years old, dirt under my nails,*
> *Throwing rocks at the bullies saying, "You're not a girl!"*
> *Scared of my own shadow*
> *I was in my own world.*
> *Longing to be free from the trap in my mind,*
> *Where the black hole of circles distorted the time.*
>
> *But I fought with a champion's heart,*
> *determined to shine.*
>
> *Days burn.*
> *Years pass.*
> *They say it gets worse before better.*
> *I found my own path.*
>
> *I wish I had seen this letter:*
>
> *You will be strong.*

You will be loved.
You will be a person
whose people are loyal and true.

Don't be scared, love!
Don't hide your face, in your hands.
Look to the sun
it's where you belong
Keep moving on.

My mom was a teacher and worked as a cartographer (someone who draws and produces maps). My dad was a cardiologist before he passed away. My dad's job as a busy doctor kept him away from home often, but he loved us very much and he sought to make a good life for us. I remember him coming home from the hospital at the end of the week with a new toy car or truck for me. On weekends after church I loved snuggling in with my head on his chest, falling asleep to the sound of his heartbeat. He was so calm that the steady beat of his warm heart helped calm the storm that was brewing inside me.

My dad grew up in a culture that was focused more on survival and practicality than understanding or expressing feelings. Because I was extra sensitive, we did not understand each other at times. He grew up in an African village and both his mom and dad passed away when he was very young. But he and his sisters were survivors. They received schooling from the missionaries; as my dad told it, he did not want to go to school at first, he wanted to hang out with the boys and go fishing and climb trees! But my oldest aunt kept my grandparents' wishes and made sure my dad attended his classes. He studied hard and this led to him eventually having his own private medical practice here in America.

He had an amazing work ethic, and he taught us that in everything we did, whether sweeping the floor or working a high level job, that we should always put in our best effort and take pride in our work. He was very even tempered and patient. One of his common sayings when things were not going our way was, "it's small potatoes." He taught me to stop and see things in perspective for what they really were. He also taught us discipline, and with just a look and a breath from him we knew when to stop misbehaving.

My dad was loving, compassionate, and generous. He would give me food right off of his plate and he would show his love by cooking me special meals. Like those Pretend-a-tips. My dad could also be stubborn and set in his ways, but he was always fair with us.

He not only obeyed God through these kind actions, he was also strong in trusting Him. One night during a terrible thunderstorm I ran into his arms. I asked, "Daddy, aren't you afraid?" He simply answered, "The only one I fear is God," meaning he didn't fear circumstances but feared disobeying God. He had the utmost reverence.

I would often come across him studying his Bible, and he would call me to come listen to a verse. He then would explain it to me until it made perfect sense. I loved his teaching. I feel I did not appreciate this until after I lost him. My dad had a deep yet kind voice, and he sang beautifully. At church I loved to hear him sing the hymns in his strong, sweet tone. His favorite hymn was "Under His Wings." My dad passed away in January of 2001. I was 24 years old. I know I will see him again in heaven one day.

My mom is warm, smart, and quick with a joke. She graduated high school at the age of 16 and went on to attend Rhode Island College. She also did graduate work at Boston University. My mom was Google before Google existed. If any of us needed to know information or how to spell something, we asked her. If she didn't know, she knew where to direct us to find out.

My mom also gives great advice. People want to talk to her, as if she is some sort of psychologist or "Dr. Mom." When I got older it sometimes seemed my friends would rather talk to her than me. She is an excellent listener and since she is so knowledgeable she follows up with wise insight and suggestions.

When I hug my mom I feel a warmth in my chest and don't want to let go. I feel safe and loved. I know she is loyal to me for life. When she tells me everything is going to be okay, I believe her.

I used to help her sort my dad's dress socks. She said she needed my young eyes to tell the blue, brown, and black socks apart. I loved that job. It made me feel important when she gave me specific tasks to complete. I took it seriously and appreciated the fact that she trusted me to give her my best.

My mom also taught me how to play cards. Not just kid games like Go Fish, but grownup games like Rummy and Double Solitaire. She never just let me win, which I appreciated. She respected me enough to let me truly play the games. I enjoyed the challenge. Particularly fun was her teaching me how to shuffle cards Vegas-style with my little hands. She doesn't like me telling people that, though—she says it makes her sound like a bad influence. She was anything but.

The bond between my mom and me could not be closer. We became a team, fighting together for my life, before autism awareness was popular. My mom was my first fan and has never stopped encouraging me in life and in all my endeavors. Like any good mom, she wanted to make it all better for me, and it made her sad when she couldn't. Today, when we talk about the past, she gets disheartened. I do too. It was a different time in the 1980s. Autism was not something doctors were mindful of or knew how to treat.

"I tried, Jennifer, I tried so hard...we just didn't know, we just couldn't figure it out," she says through tears.

I know how hard my mom tried and how much she wished she could have fixed it. But how could she know what she didn't know?

I was very close to my older brothers, who are 18 months apart. They are six and seven years older than me, and as a child I wanted to be able to do everything that they could do. They patiently let me tag along through the neighborhood as long as I could keep up. It was difficult on my Big Wheel... but I tried.

They also were—well—big brothers who enjoyed teasing and playing pranks on me. Including hiding my favorite lamb puppet in the freezer on Easter morning—claiming it was dinner—and locking me in the basement when my mom wasn't home. Don't worry, it wasn't as bad as it sounds. Technically our basement had a sliding glass door through which I could have gotten out. But that would mean I would have to run past the boiler room, where I was certain the devil lived. If I ran by that room, I just knew a devil hand would grab me and take me away, so instead I cried on the stairway until they felt bad enough to let me out.

Even though I would get upset at my brothers' shenanigans, I seemed to know it came from a place of love. I seemed to know they loved *ME*. I came back for more. They made me feel part of everything when they played tricks on me. They treated me just like any other little sister.

Sometimes my brothers would take the time to stop and play with me. This didn't always go well, since they didn't know how to follow my rules, but they tried to understand my quirks and were there to love and protect me. In the fall, we often built leaf piles to jump in. We went sledding in the winter. One hot summer night, we built a fort out of sheets and put a fan inside, making our own refreshing tent to sleep in.

One December, an enormous box appeared under the tree with my name on it. My curiosity was insatiable. When I shook it, it was heavy and seemed to have many parts inside. That present became my focus until Christmas morning. I tore into that gift first. I got it open, peered inside, and there were...shoes. Several pairs of old, smelly shoes. I didn't understand. I looked around at my family's faces for a clue. First my mom, then my dad, started scolding my brother, yelling, "How could you do that to your sister?" I started to cry at the commotion, but I still had faith in my brother.

As the chastising continued, I started pulling out all of the shoes. My brother kept saying to my parents, "No, wait! Look!" Just then I saw it. At the bottom of this stinky-shoe box was the most beautiful gold Matchbox racing car I had ever seen. It had a number 8 painted on the hood and it was *perfect*. I grabbed it, jumped up, and hugged my brother. I was so happy to get that car.

My parents were still upset with him for tricking me, but I was unaffected by his joke. Even though my brother was in trouble, he was happy that I was happy. Though I started out confused, I didn't stay that way. I no longer saw the prank; I just saw the goodness in him. We understood each other. When my brothers teased, they showed me love. They didn't spoil or baby me.

They didn't treat me differently. They loved me. Besides all this, they helped toughen me up, which I would need later in life.

My sister is fourteen years older than I am, so we weren't as close growing up. She is spunky, energetic, funny, and thoughtful. She has the most beautiful singing voice. I remember when she would play the guitar and sing hymns, her rich tone resonated in my bones just right. My sister also introduced me to my first favorite band: New Edition. We would dance and sing to that cassette tape until it wore out. I was always a tomboy and she was a girly girl, but still we built a great relationship and I love her. I have an old picture of her fixing me a bottle when I was young. I was wearing a little outfit my siblings lovingly called "the pear suit" because it made me look, well, just like a pear. My sister taught me that it's okay to dance like nobody's watching.

As a unit, my family has a love for laughter. A lot of times my dad would miss the joke...then slowly his face would break into a smile as he unravelled the punchline, and that would make us laugh even more, this time all together. My parents always made Christmas and holidays special, and I have fond memories of these times (even the one with the gold car mixed with smelly shoes).

On church mornings, being the youngest I remember I was always the last one to get a shower. It became a competition to see who could get to the shower first. Sometimes if my brother started the water so it would heat up, the other one would jump in, stealing all the hot water. I learned to be quick on my feet and always alert in my house because I never knew when I might get bamboozled...in a loving way.

We would have arguments too, of course. My brothers would complain and get annoyed because my dad didn't make me do yard work. We would often "borrow" each other's things without asking, sometimes leading to an all-out shouting match, and my parents sometimes disagreed about grownup things. I would hear them speaking heatedly in hushed tones. But at the end of the day, we all love each other very much and stick by each other like family should.

CHAPTER 3

A Super Creative Kid

"I liked to make special birthday cards for my family that were interactive with doors to open and roads to drive toy cars on."

I was a super creative kid. I enjoyed making things out of paper and tape. I would roll up pieces of paper and make them into little play people, complete with interchangeable outfits. I also liked to make special interactive birthday cards for my family, with doors to open and roads to drive toy cars on. I even started a family newspaper in which I would write all the articles, ads, and comics (mostly jokes about my brothers) and then try to sell them for twenty-five cents. My family was not interested in paying for my literary efforts, and the *Msumba Magnificent* only lasted for three issues.

For some reason I was obsessed with casts—like the kind you get for a broken arm. I would wet paper towels and wrap them around the limbs of my stuffed animals. I was also fascinated with football and I would stuff my sleeves with tissues to make shoulder pads and use a belt to strap an empty margarine container on my head for a helmet. Then I would ram my head into the side of my parents' bed repeatedly as if I were an offensive lineman. The head banging concerned my mom, and she asked me if it hurt. It did. But it also appeared to soothe me, so she let me play my game.

I also loved to play with LEGO, building blocks, and Matchbox cars (including the beautiful golden one from my brother). I would play with these tiny items for hours while my parents read nearby. When my brothers weren't around, I liked to play alone. My guess is I did that because no one else understood my rules. I would make games out of ordinary things no one else noticed. The dust particles floating in the sunbeam coming through the big picture windows in the living room entranced me. I would follow them with my eyes and then try to catch my favorite ones. I loved this game so much that I had trouble pulling away from it when it was time to go to school. I would cry and beg my mom to let me stay home. It appeared I was being defiant, but I just wanted to continue my game.

I love music—listening to it and playing it. I now play the guitar, piano, violin, ukulele, and bass guitar. I grew up listening to my parents' records—a mixture of hymns and classical music with the occasional Roberta Flack or Carly Simon. The classical music made me dance on the inside. I would find myself moving my eyes as if they were a conductor's baton, and hum and breathe to the varying tempos of Handel, Vivaldi and Bach. I quickly memorized the order of the tracks on the records, and always knew which song was coming on next. I would sometimes pick out on my xylophone little tunes I had heard.

When my parents weren't home, my brothers would play Michael Jackson's "Thriller" or Pat Benatar, so I got to sample a wide variety of genres. I listened as I played with my cars and trucks in the living room.

When I was three years old, my dad surprised the family with a brand new piano. I clearly remember the men hauling it into the living room one Saturday evening. My brothers and I were so excited! Of course, they pushed ahead of me and got to play it first but they tired of it quickly and then I got my chance. I remember trying to play the songs I had heard in church and on our records.

I was systematic in exploring the keys, and didn't just bang them to make noise. I wanted to make beautiful music. Soon one brother started piano lessons, and my mom brought me along to wait for him. Sitting on the flowery living room couch while playing with the Colorforms his teacher gave me, I could hear him playing the same song, "Minuet in G," over and over. One day, after his lesson, I ran and sat at her piano. She asked me if I wanted to learn. Yes I did! My mom signed me up.

Wanting to be like my brother, of course the first song I wanted to learn was "Minuet in G." Our teacher showed me some simple books, teaching me all the notes in a scale. I learned quickly. Music was logical. It had a set of rules and I liked that. When I followed those rules, the notes created beautiful shapes and sound waves. It made so much sense to me. The differences in the notes were distances I could see. The corresponding spaces made notes in my mind. I didn't really need the music once I heard the song, because my mind made a map for me to follow. My brother was angry that his little sister had beat him at learning "Minuet in G." I had finally beat him at something! I felt proud. While I liked the structure of the music itself, I didn't like the structure of the lessons or practicing songs. I ended up quitting after about six months. But don't worry. That was not the end of my music career.

My brothers started playing the trumpet in school and I really wanted to play with them. I remember my mom and dad bought me a little plastic silver trumpet that only played one note and I used to squeeze in between my brothers, saying, "Move! Can't see moo-sic!" They called me "Jenny One Note." My brothers were patient with me and let me play my little one-note trumpet with them as they practiced. Everyone figured that when I was old enough for the school band, I would play the trumpet too.

But did I have a curveball for them! One day in third grade, the teachers sat us down in the middle of the room and three music teachers came in. Without saying a word, they arranged their chairs in a semicircle and pulled out beautiful wooden instruments—a violin, a viola, and a cello. From them came the most glorious music. I was mesmerized. They played Pachelbel's "Canon in D." I marveled at the way all three instruments produced music that danced around each other. Each teacher played a different line, but they fit together like a brilliant tapestry, a puzzle that created a perfect picture. My ears were keen to the beauty and I was in love. The violin in particular impressed me. Its tones reached out in a rushing wave of vibrations that entered my chest. I *needed* that violin. I came running home with my little permission slip. My mom couldn't believe I wanted to play such a delicate instrument but I was adamant. I knew it was for me. My parents, not being the type to squash our creative dreams, said yes.

The violin ended up being my saving grace in elementary school. I excelled at it. My teacher told my mom he believed I had perfect pitch. Playing the violin was my time of peace at school. I looked forward to every Tuesday and Thursday when I would get excused from other classes for my lessons. We practiced in a sunny, quiet corner by the cafeteria. Our teacher was thorough but patient. He wanted excellence and I was there to achieve that. I found a place where I felt safe at school. I belonged. No bullies. No teachers putting me down. Just beautiful, intricate music. By the time I was in sixth grade I was promoted into the high school's All Town Orchestra. My violin teacher was proud of me, and I felt proud of myself. Music would later grow to become an even larger part of my life.

CHAPTER 4

Fears, Tics, and Obsessions– My Over-and-Overs

"Shout at the leaves!"

When I was in second grade, I was outside on my driveway riding my bike in circles. This activity soothed me, along with repeating words and phrases as I glided around. Out of nowhere, I had an intense urge to roll my eyes in the back of my head and squeeze until it hurt. I did it, and then the urge went away.

That was weird, I thought to myself and went back to riding my bike. Then the feeling came back, and I felt I had to do it again. Then again. I had no idea what was happening to my body, and I felt little to no control over these eye rolls.

When I went back to the house that afternoon, the urges continued. Out of shame and fear, I made certain no one saw my new habit. I went to sleep that night feeling optimistic. Things always felt better in the morning and I concluded that, just as quickly as this eye rolling all started, it would stop.

* * * * *

I don't know why I felt shame and fear. Maybe I would have felt less lonely if I had told someone. I trusted my mom, but I felt that she wouldn't understand what I was going through. I was embarrassed of myself. But looking back, I wish I had reached out and taken that chance. I've learned that we are almost never alone in our feelings or struggles and that talking about them helps immensely. Even if my mom didn't understand, she wouldn't have stopped until she helped me find the answer, possibly saving me years of suffering. In the same way I implore you to find your loyal and true people. You will know who they are because they will still be your people even when you have nothing to offer. They will stick by you even after you have made mistakes. They will show you true care rather than hurt you. These are people you can trust the most. If it is too hard to tell them your struggles verbally, try writing a note about what you are going through and ask for help. Asking for help takes humility, which is a positive attribute to develop.

* * * * *

Morning came and the eye rolls continued. Soon they were joined by a new urge to close off my throat to make a choking feeling. I would create this feeling by tightening my throat, holding that position until it felt enough, and then letting go. I may have perfected a technique that served my urges, but eating became tricky. Eating triggered the urge to close off my throat. That meant I couldn't swallow. Sometimes I would almost actually choke on my food.

I kept this all a secret because I was confused and embarrassed. Why was I doing these things? Why was I hurting myself? Would I ever be able to stop? What if the urges never went away?

Before I knew it, I was also contorting my arms and back while tightening my muscles until it hurt. I held that and then let go.

I couldn't stop these things from happening, and I was ashamed of myself. I felt hopeless. These actions hurt my body and I wasn't sure I could hide it from people much longer.

I became a pro at dodging behind furniture or out of sight to do each tic or obsession. I was very good at keeping these movements a secret from my family, friends and teachers. I recently found some old family videos where I was performing these contortions. I watched my eight-year-old self as I ran behind my mom and brother and did my tic. I desperately wanted to keep this a secret until it went away. I'm not sure why. I believed it would stop just as quickly as it started.

Later in life I would learn that these tics were related to Obsessive Compulsive Disorder and Autism.

While I was trying to manage the tics, I developed some intense fears, obsessions, and rituals. I called them my overs-and-overs. I grew up going to church, so I had a basic understanding of God and the devil. My brain took this information and distorted it into a nightmare. I became convinced that the devil was hiding around the corners in the house and had a big, long hand that could reach out, grab me, and take me away to a scary place. The fear became so intense that I couldn't go anywhere at night without clinging tightly to a family member. One night, my mom was trying to clean the garage and I was out there with her, grasping her shirt. My mischievous older brother decided he was going to jump out and scare me from behind the door. He was just being a typical brother, but I screamed, cried, and then clutched even more tightly onto my mom. She could barely move. Infuriated, she told my brother she didn't want to see his face the rest of the night. Now with my clinging, my mother's work got even harder.

After my brother left I started to quiet down, but my mind was still reeling. I was terrified. All of a sudden, I clearly heard a male voice say, "Jennifer, do not be afraid." It was the most beautiful voice I have ever heard. I stopped in my tracks, trying to process. But my fear took back over and I started to cry. I said, "Mom, he's teasing me again." My mom looked up to scold my brother, only he wasn't there. She went into the kitchen, and he wasn't there either. Finally, she called downstairs to the basement family room, and my brother answered. He was so far away that it was impossible I had heard his voice. When my mom confronted him, he honestly had no idea what she was talking about. Minute by minute, I figured out that the voice did not belong to my brother, but to God. I felt that it was hurting God to see me so afraid, so He spoke to me. I have held onto those sweet words ever since.

Around the same time, I started developing more and more irrational fears of items and actions. I remember one specific fear of soap, particularly shampoo. Somehow I got the idea in my head that if I didn't rinse all of the shampoo out of my hair before I put on the conditioner, there would be a chemical reaction between the shampoo and conditioner, resulting in an explosion on my head. I know it seems silly, but I was thoroughly convinced this was a fact.

I was old enough that my mom was no longer monitoring my showers. She still had to tell me to go take one, which I hated. But I started just standing under the running water until enough time had passed and then I would get out and get in my pajamas. I would not touch the soap or wash my hair. This went on for quite some time before I got caught. One of my brothers got a whiff of my hair one day and told my mom that I smelled. I was ashamed and embarrassed.

After that, my mom marched me to the shower and I admitted to her my fear. Again, why didn't I tell her in the first place? She would have saved me weeks and weeks of panic. I can't stress enough to never worry alone. My mom was able to convince me that shampoo and conditioner could not explode.

Slowly I got over my fear. Today, ironically, I use 2-in-1 shampoo and conditioner. According to my kid logic, that would make it a bomb in a bottle!

To this day, I am still not a fan of showers. Don't get me wrong, I like being clean, and I love the feeling after I'm dry and dressed. However, I flinch at the sensation of first getting into the shower and the water hitting me. After I'm wet and start scrubbing, I actually enjoy showering. Then I resist it again when it's time to get out. It's the whole transition process that I hate. Being wet is fine. Being dry is fine. But being dry and then wet feels strange. Being wet, then damp, then dry, and then having to put clothes back on feels uncomfortable. I despise the feeling of being wet when I'm not completely in the water.

* * * * *

Your feelings of discomfort may match mine or may be all your own. But tell a caring somebody. Oftentimes parents can be helpful, but sometimes not. They may not recognize your needs, especially as you get older and they assume you should be able to care more for yourself. This may happen because they don't know how to help or because they choose not to see. There are other reasons as well. If this is your case, you can still find people who will help you. This could be a friend or another family member that you trust. Let them help you manage it. You are not alone.

* * * * *

Little by little I had to find ways to manage my fears, obsessions, and rituals—my over-and-overs. I don't want to communicate that anyone has much control over OCD and other over-and-overs. But I did need to choose to come out of the dark place of sadness and fear. A turning point for me was both a help and a foreshadowing: I had to learn to shout at the leaves.

Every fall, my older brothers and I would play in the fallen leaves from the twin oak in our front yard. I loved when my brothers buried me under the leaves we raked up. I enjoyed the warmth and darkness under there, with only muffled sounds from the outside world. I felt safe under the weight of the leaves. But those dusty leaves also made it hard to breathe. If I stayed under there too long, I would cough and choke. Hearing me sputter, my brothers would shout at me to unbury myself and come up for air. Once I did, the cool air would hit my face and I would take a deep breath. Wiping my eyes, I would notice how bright the autumn colors were in the sunlight. It was like seeing the world for the first time. What a refreshment!!

Staying buried isn't conducive to life. One definition of *buried* is "covered up, or repressed." Little did I know that my future would have me buried in darkness, struggling to find light and life. My brothers couldn't save me during those times. I was going to have to shout at those leaves and save myself.

* * * * *

I've told you about my tics and intense fears. What came next? Cue the obsessions. The day my obsessions began, I felt like I became encased in a glass bottle. I could see out, and people could see me, but there was a thick syrupy layer between the world and me. That day was a school holiday, the weather was rainy, and I was watching TV. My brother would run a race at his prep school that day and we were all going to watch him. Before that could happen, the obsessions fell on me. The pressure felt like one of those gloppy rain clouds had made its way inside the house and landed right on top of my head. I was intensely burdened. I felt insurmountable feelings of guilt over insignificant things. Both my mind and my body felt weighed down and my internal joy was separated from me, as if outside that glass.

I thought this pressure would go away if I could just distract myself. I was excited about my brother's race so I tried to reclaim that joy I had been feeling just minutes earlier. But I couldn't grab it. It stayed just out of reach.

I stood in the cool mist among the crowd as they cheered the racers, but it was as if I wasn't there. I was buried inside glass. Again, I believed these feelings and thoughts would go away just as fast as they came on. Only they didn't. They just grew worse and worse.

I developed rituals. A ritual can be logical; for example, brushing your teeth every morning or eating meals three times a day. But mine were driven by compulsion or inaccuracies. So when I say I developed a ritual, it wasn't like I sat down and planned it out with a rational mind. Each ritual developed a life of its own. The ritual was born from false beliefs and grew when I fed it with compulsions. I couldn't control the ritual; it controlled me.

I started forcing my family to participate in my rituals. For example I was convinced my mom would die in a car accident every time she went somewhere without me. I developed a goodbye ritual that took fifteen minutes to complete. It included prayers, repeating words, telling her to wear her seat belt, and saying "I love you" a certain number of times. Then I asked her if she knew that I loved her. She then had to repeat certain things back to me. If there was an interruption in the process, we had to start over.

My mom was not a fan of the goodbye ritual, but she did it because she knew it made me feel better and because it was the only way I could relax when we were apart. When it first began, she tried to assure me that the routine wasn't necessary to keep her safe, but that did not register with me. She learned early on that resisting the ritual created more work for her to be able to soothe me when she was leaving. The goodbye ritual became a staple in my home.

I would also obsess over any objects or gifts my mom gave me. I believed that, if they ever got broken or lost, my mom would die and it would be all my fault. She used to buy cute little erasers for me at a downtown shop and I would carry them carefully in a pencil case to and from school. I never actually used them to erase anything. Sometimes I would take them out and hold them to feel closer to my mom. One day in third grade, I left my new calculator eraser on my desk. It was blue with great detail including buttons and a tiny on/off switch. Suddenly, it was gone. I panicked. Looking around, I saw some boys giggling at their desks. I knew who had taken my eraser. I remember his first and last name to this day. I went to take it back from him, but he held on tight. We wrestled over it but he was a big boy and I lost. Finally, I went to tell my teacher what had happened. That's when he threw my eraser back at me. It bounced off my back and hit the floor. Relieved, I snatched it up off the floor and ran to my desk to inspect the damage. Tears rushed to my eyes as I saw that he had used it to erase his work and had also broken off the tiny on/off switch.

I was so sad. I was worried that my mom would think I didn't love her and that she would get into an accident before I could get home and apologize. I couldn't concentrate the rest of the day until I got home and went through the "I'm sorry" ritual with my mom to keep her safe.

* * * * *

I also stopped being able to sleep. I would be up worrying about a fire in the house, or bad people hurting us at night. I would get up, turn on all the lights as I ran downstairs (quickly to avoid the devil's hands), and check the locks on the doors. I would unlock each door, then lock it again. But then I couldn't trust my eyes, so I would unlock and lock again.

Did my eyes really see it right that time?

Was it locked?

Then again.

And again, and again, and again.

I became, what I call, "stuck." Onto the outlets. I would unplug the toaster, the microwave—any appliance where I could reach the plug. I would unplug them, *see* they were unplugged, but I couldn't believe that they were. Then I would plug them back in so that my eyes could watch the plugs come out of the sockets. Over and over.

Are you getting tired yet? I am. I was so tired but I couldn't stop. Many nights, my dad would wake up and catch me doing this. He would try to reassure me and get me back to bed. He would promise to check all the locks and outlets, and check the basement for fires if I would go back to bed. He was so patient with me but I knew he was concerned.

Still, I couldn't sleep.

So I would just lay in bed with the lights on, listening for bad men and smelling for smoke.

* * * * *

One of my obsessions as I got older was with a popular band called Bon Jovi. This may have seemed like a normal obsession for a girl my age, but it became too all-consuming for me. I focused on Bon Jovi to keep my world in order. I would watch MTV constantly for their music videos, and I talked about them all the time, repeating every fact I knew about them. Was I ever excited when I saw the advertisement for Bon Jovi weekend on MTV! Friday came, and I rushed home from school and flipped on my small TV. The screen was all scrambled, a telltale sign that the cable was out. I ran downstairs to tell my mom about the television, and while rinsing dishes in the sink, she nonchalantly let me know that she had blocked MTV because I was becoming too obsessed.

I lost it. I believed my entire world crumbled. Bon Jovi was keeping my world together. Now my glue was gone without warning. It was the element of surprise that really pulled the rug out from under me. I melted down. I didn't even know what to do with my body. I ran around the house, throwing myself into walls, banging my head. I felt no pain. I couldn't control it. This wasn't a temper tantrum. I didn't even want it to be happening, but it was. My brother was following me around the house, trying to shield me from hurting myself. He and my mom didn't know what to do. Hours later, I finally calmed down. Then I fell asleep hard.

My obsessions, rituals, and intrusive thoughts barreled down on me like a freight train. I felt like I was being held captive, and I could no longer find peace except for the few seconds after I would perform a ritual. For those few seconds, everything would go away and I felt elated and relieved. I called it my "five seconds of peace." Then the train would come barreling back and I would be right back in the endless loop. I would try to fight off the painful thoughts with other loops of words. I would repeat to myself quietly, "OK, OK, OK, alright, alright, alright." I repeated these words to try and cover up the bad thoughts and urges. This endless loop became both my nemesis and my comfort.

CHAPTER 5
Friends and School, Part 1

*"I knew what I wanted to express but the words
disappeared before I could verbalize them."*

My first friends were two girls who lived in my neighborhood. Shannon and
Carol were the same age as me, and our moms were friends. We would often
go for swimming lessons together and then go out to eat at Denny's. We were
together so frequently that we played together a lot. Shannon always seemed
more mature than her age and had a calm and motherly demeanor. She had
curly hair like mine, which made me feel less alone with my head full of
tight curls. I trusted Shannon, she was protective of me, and I allowed her to
make the rules. She always got to decide what we played. She made me play
the board game Clue before she would agree to ride bikes with me. I had no
idea what I was doing in that game, so I always picked Professor Plum in the
billiard room with the candlestick. Then we could go ride bikes!

Carol and I were hot and cold, more like frenemies than friends. We
were forced to interact but did not like each other. She loved all things girly
and pink, and the teachers thought she was a saint. She wasn't. One time she
scratched me across the face during a disagreement and left a scar. Her mom
would do her school projects for her, and then the teachers would give her
all sorts of rewards and recognition for them, making us clap for her as she
went onstage to receive her certificates. The injustice of it all! It frustrated me.
Most of it was because the work was not hers. Part of it was I never received
awards, especially since I was seen as a troublemaker in my school.

I was not a bad kid, but I was often singled out and blamed for things
because of my impulsive tendencies. I had a hard time controlling my emotions in class, and was known for running out into the hall and hiding in the

coat racks or stairway when I felt angry, sad, or embarrassed. This didn't win me points with the teachers. When we got an electric pencil sharpener for our class, which was a big deal in the '80s, we were lectured on how expensive it was and how we were not to put any objects except pencils in it. Soon enough someone jammed a yellow crayon into the sharpener...and I was blamed.

Then Carol's pink winter jacket got shoved into the toilet in the girls' bathroom, and again, I was blamed. I can see why someone did it because other people also had to notice her cruelty, but I had nothing to do with these crimes. The injustice of being accused made me red hot. Kids teased me even more for getting in trouble, and it really hurt my heart.

I am bi-racial. I have brown skin and very curly hair, and I really stood out in my predominantly white school. In kindergarten, my (white) mom came to school, where the other kids saw her. Until this point, I had not noticed I was different. I didn't even notice that my *parents* were different colors, until the other kids pointed it out. They started teasing me, saying that I was adopted because my white mom "couldn't be my real mom." I went home crying, unable to articulate what had happened. I was ashamed of my dark skin. I remember grabbing a box of white chalk and scribbling it all over my hands. My mom broke down in tears. She hugged me tight and we cried together. Afterward, she told me to never, ever be ashamed of my beautiful brown skin. That was going to be a hard task.

I was one of the only kids who could read in my kindergarten class. But I was behind in other things. Our teacher, Mrs. Harris, had two big blocks with laces in them that were made for learning shoe tying. I tried so hard, but I just couldn't grasp the concept. My little hands wouldn't listen to me. My mind would coax them to follow the pattern of instructions, but my fingers felt more tied up than my shoes ever got. Soon all the kids had mastered this skill but me. My teacher, frustrated, made me stay in from recess so I could work on it. I felt singled out—it felt like a punishment—so I came up with my own alternate method of tying shoes so that I could go out to recess. I used a clumsy technique of loops and knots to achieve my goal. Again, I was learning how to adapt in a frustrating world. Finally she gave up on me, accepted my alternate (and very inefficient) way of tying shoes, and I was back out at recess, playing with my little cars in the sandbox.

My daily bus ride was the worst. There was one particular boy, Tim, who made a point of seeking me out to torment me on a daily basis. He called me the N word, and he would take little pieces of paper and stick them in my hair to get the other kids to laugh. He made me sick to my stomach—and furious—every time I saw him. I felt red hot inside. I wanted to punch him but couldn't muster up the courage. I felt alone. I was puzzled about how someone could be so cruel for no reason. I had no concept of this as I couldn't stand to see others hurt. Tim was the meanest kid I ever knew.

When we arrived at school, we played on the playground until the morning bell. I looked forward to recess because being outside made me feel free—like the squirrels I enjoyed watching, chasing each other around our big oak tree. The outside air was soft on my ears and the colors were natural and unintrusive. It was also when the bullies had a free-for-all. Most of the bullies in my school were boys who would taunt me, saying I looked like a boy with my Toughskins corduroys. They mocked my short, curly hair and brown skin. They called me stupid and ugly.

All this rightly stirred up a fighting spirit in me. I remember getting really hot inside and wanting to defend myself. My mother tried to instill in me that I was bright and beautiful. So, in my mind, they were also hurting my mom. I had to defend *her*. My anger got to the point where I couldn't even see anymore. Then I burst. The closest thing I had to throw at them were rocks. So I started hurling them at the mean boys. I have an accurate throwing arm and the bullies ran away, scared and shocked that I fought back. *Good,* I thought. *Maybe now they will leave me alone.*

The only problem was that I had been spotted by one of the recess monitors. As a punishment, I had to spend recess sitting on a bench by myself for a period of time. I was also brought to the principal's office and she grilled me for what seemed like hours. All I could do was shrug my shoulders and say, "I don't know." I wanted to tell her. Everything in me wanted to tell her about the mean boys teasing me, but the words would not come. I knew what I wanted to express, but the words disappeared before I could verbalize them.

Time and time again this extremely frustrating scenario played itself out. I was a whole person inside. I had deep feelings I wanted to share. I wanted to express my pain. I even wanted to connect with others when I saw *their* pain. But all I could say was, "I don't know."

* * * * *

I soon discovered I wasn't the only one in my family with a fighting spirit. One summer day toward the end of my kindergarten year, our young art teacher decided to leave the classroom unattended for several minutes. When the other kids realized this, they began throwing crayons and running around the room like wild little rabbits. I was elected, along with a boy named Sammy, by our peers to watch the door. Longing to be liked and fit in, I accepted this position with honor. Sammy and I stood at that door, keeping our eyes peeled on the hallway for our teacher's telltale Birkenstock sandals.

But she was too fast. She must have heard the ruckus from down the hall and came bustling in the door, catching us off guard. Sammy was quicker than I was and, unfortunately, I was the first kid she saw. She grabbed me by the shoulder and squeezed me tight, shaking me like a ragdoll. I could feel droplets of her spit hit my face as she screamed at me. After she let go to take back control of the room, I could feel my shoulder throbbing. I was in shock and pain but I didn't cry.

My mom picked me up and I climbed in the car with her. Still in the school driveway, she asked me how my day was. I could not process what had happened and again, words escaped me. All I could do was point to my shoulder. She anxiously pulled down my shirt collar, revealing four clear fingermark bruises. I winced in pain. Words came out of her mouth that I had never heard her say before. I was terrified to see her so angry. I thought I had done something wrong, so I started to cry. She took me by the hand and we marched back into the school. My little legs could barely keep up with her angry strides. She barged into the principal's office and angrily pointed out my injury to her.

I was then sent to sit outside with the kind secretary. Her un-intimidating demeanor was a safe contrast to our bristly principal. I think we were both afraid of what was going down in that office. I still thought I had done something wrong. Mom came out of the office calmer, but still wearing her 'mama bear' face. I started to cry again and told her I was sorry. She then explained that I hadn't done anything wrong but my teacher had acted inappropriately. She explained that no one was allowed to hurt me and that I should always tell her if someone does and she would protect me. The next year, we had a new art teacher.

CHAPTER 6

Friends and School, Part 2

"I loved most of my academic subjects, especially math."

Mrs. Simpson, my library teacher, made a lasting impression on me, but not in a good way. She was older but not grandmotherly. She was terse and took her position seriously in all the wrong ways. The Dewey Decimal System was her maxim. The card catalog was law, and you didn't want to be *booked* into library jail by breaking her rules. In the beginning of first grade, most kids in my class could not read yet. When we had library time, Mrs. Simpson would read us a book, and afterward direct us to books we could look at. To my dismay, they were all picture books! I quickly became bored and wandered into the older kids' section that had books with words and chapters. This was hardly a crime the way I see it, but she got very angry. She marched me back to the picture book section and made me sit in what she called the baby chair. She announced to the whole class this was my punishment because I didn't listen.

The chair was a yellow cube that came from the kindergarten class, rumored to have been peed on. This shame-based approach to discipline was hurtful to my young heart. Because she was a grownup, I believed it when she called me a baby. In turn, I started acting out more because I didn't think I was valuable in her world or in the world in general. Mrs. Simpson and I continued to clash for the next six years. Eventually I refused to go to library class. When my kind fifth grade teacher took the time to ask me why, all I could muster was a shrug and, "I don't know." I wanted to tell her about wanting to read books and the baby chair Mrs. Simpson punished me with, but the words wouldn't come. All these years, I wasn't able to communicate feelings with my family, and it was becoming painfully obvious that I couldn't build relationships with my teachers either.

I was still inside my glass bottle but it was getting thicker. I wanted to reach through it and pour out my soul, but I was stuck, and didn't know what to do about it.

* * * * *

Even amidst the struggles with teachers and bullies, there were still things about school I enjoyed. I loved most of my academic subjects, especially math. It was logical and had strict rules. Math made me feel light, and I didn't have to use words or feelings to communicate my answers. Numbers and symbols were exact in their meaning. They presented no surprises. Because math is black and white, I didn't feel the weight of the gray realm— the realm of words, feelings, and emotions.

Gym class was epic in my young world. In my mind, I could throw and catch like Wade Boggs from the Red Sox. My mom loves the Red Sox, and she was the one who taught me to be the best third baseman Little League had ever seen. In gym class, we would play a modified dodgeball game... much less brutal than your classic ball-stinging-your-face version so popular in the 1980s. I usually got picked first for teams because gym class wasn't a popularity contest. Kids just wanted to win. When the team captain would call my name, I felt accepted and light as I jogged over to my teammates. Gym was invigorating. Using my muscles to throw, catch, dodge, and run was a major release of tension.

I did *not* feel the same sentiment for square dancing. Our class usually didn't have an equal number of boys and girls. One of the gym teachers, Mr. Huxley, was cruel. He made us do squat thrusts until kids threw up. I knew the key to avoiding his wrath was to follow his instructions, but not when it came time for square dancing.

We all loathed that record player commanding us to do-si-do and bow to our partner. Inevitably, and to even up partners, Mr. Huxley made me wear a yellow pinny to signify I was dancing the boy partner's role. The kids would laugh and point at me. I don't know his reason for singling me out, but I was mortified. It was bad enough I was singled out for being bi-racial; now I was on display for not having a boy partner. Feeling red hot inside, I would run out of class and hide in the coat racks. They would send the school counselor after me to find out why I ran off, as if you needed a degree in psychology to see what could possibly be wrong with this scenario.

* * * * *

Christy was my mud-slinging/forest-exploring/creek-swimming best friend. She was easy-going and didn't mind playing by Jen's Epic Book of Gametime Management. In other words, she did not make me play Clue. She played by my rules. She even agreed to play on the eight-year-old Little League baseball team, knowing we would be the only two girls.

Two games into the season I broke my arm, leaving her as the only female member on the team. Our dynamic duo stayed together for four years. The day Christy traded in her ball cap for pom-poms was the beginning of the end. Soon after she became a cheerleader, she stopped wanting to play with me. I felt abandoned by one of only two friends who had truly seemed to understand me (Shannon was the other). This was my first taste of what happens as girls get older and start to form cliques. Christy was no longer interested in riding bikes or playing in the mud. She wasn't mean to me after that; she just found new friends and ignored me. She seemed to be maturing faster than I was. She treated me like she never even knew me. I felt lost.

CHAPTER 7

Friends and School, Part 3

"I felt licensed to be me. I belonged. I was embraced. I felt alive."

The summer after third grade, when my mom started signing me up for day camp, I was less than thrilled. She said I wasn't going to spend the whole summer playing by myself. Though I had been perfectly happy, riding my bike in circles, she wanted me to interact more.

The first day of day camp, I was sure I would come face to face with a new pack of bullies from the other side of town. At least at school I knew if I hung out under the trees (where the perfect throwing rocks were located) I would be safe from Tim and his sidekicks. When I got out of the car on my first day with my little lunch box and towel, I shut down at the first sight of the other kids. The 20-foot journey from car to campground was a rough 15 minutes for all involved. The camp counselors quickly jumped in and distracted me with crafts and games which included throwing and catching—my favorite!

Later that day I made a small group of friends. These kids had behavior issues or took medicine for ADHD. This was the first time I felt like I truly belonged because they were seen as different like I was. Here at camp, there were no divisions and I was able to bond with kids who felt like I did. As outsiders, we had been underestimated and misunderstood. What people didn't know was that we were energetic, creative, and accepting. We chose no judgment. I was happy to be included in this group because I felt like I could relax. My anxiety decreased while my confidence increased. These peers did not ask me questions like why my mom was white. They actually approached me and asked me to play with them. They seemed unphased by my lack of social skills. They did not care if I had a Benetton jacket. They did not ridicule me for off-brand shoes. They did not seem affected when I looked at the ground while we talked. They saw me as a person and I felt licensed to be me. I belonged. I was embraced. I felt alive.

Even though I was accepted and cherished at camp, my tics were becoming more violent and difficult to hide. Camp was a good distraction. We played games like Heads Up, Seven Up and Duck, Duck, Goose. We made lanyards and went swimming at the pond every day. I brought my little money from my piggybank to buy popsicles or Jolly Rancher sticks from the snack shop. The older kids would push us on the merry-go-round and I learned to jump off before it got going too fast. On Fridays we would grill hot dogs and roast marshmallows.

After swimming in the pond, we would get changed to walk back to the campsite. I was a slow dresser because I had rituals of not touching the wet floor in the bathroom. Also my hands seemed to get confused when I tried to pull my shirt on or do my buttons. Consequently I was always the last one to be ready.

On top of that, I still couldn't tie my shoes. Everyone would have to wait for me. The counselors would often tie my shoes for me to hurry things up, but one day one of them got sick of it. He told me that he was going to teach me to tie my shoes. When we got back to the campground, the counselors and older kids worked with me on tying. They encouraged me and showed me over and over again. Finally, finally, I had a breakthrough! Shoe tying suddenly made sense to me and I got my hands to listen to me. I tied my shoes! I was so excited. Everyone cheered, I felt like a star. Take that, Mrs. Harris!!

CHAPTER 8

Friends and School, Part 4

"I was knocked backwards by the noise and commotion."

My wonderful camp experience was the summer before fourth grade. Once school began, my day went something like this:

Each morning my mom had a difficult time waking me. I hadn't slept well due to my obsessive thoughts and rituals keeping me awake most of the night before. I was busy locking doors and checking for fires. I had trouble staying asleep and feared the devil's hands would grab me in the dark.

After the struggle to get out of bed, I would slowly get dressed and ready because I have trouble initiating those actions. My mom would often find me standing in my room, frozen, proclaiming that I didn't know what to do next. She later realized that I needed step-by-step directions when completing longer tasks. All this made us late for school and my mom had to drive me. I hated the bus, so this was hardly a bad thing in my mind.

Arriving in class, I was knocked backward by the noise and commotion. The setup of my school was different from most schools. It was an open concept where almost all one hundred students in the grade were taught in one big loft. These lofts were long and consisted of three classrooms each, with no walls or dividers between them. While we tried to learn language arts, a science class went on right next to us where we could hear and see everything. I found it much more interesting to watch kids making volcanoes erupt than to learn parts of speech. On top of this, the noise and chaos between class times was insurmountable for me to handle because of my sensory issues. This was known to my teachers, but the only option for a closed classroom was to be placed in special ed. I didn't qualify due to my high academic level, and I didn't want to qualify. I wanted to stay with the mainstream group.

Still I pressed on, wishing I was at home catching sunlit dust. As my math teacher spoke, my mind suddenly latched on to the thought that my mom could get into a car accident while I was at school. It would be all my fault because in our rush, I didn't have time to do the goodbye ritual thoroughly that morning. I pushed this thought to one side of my brain while I used the other side to focus on the teacher's question, "How do you find the circumference of a circle?" *Ooh, I know this!* I raised my hand eagerly and the teacher looked right at me. She then shifted her gaze right over my head to Carol and called on her for the answer. Carol answered smugly, aware she was the teacher's favorite student. The teacher praised her as if no one else knew the answer. Hot inside with frustration, my eagerness to learn dwindled little by little.

As the teacher droned on, my mind switched back to obsessing. My brain insisted that I *wanted* my mom to die in a car accident.

No, I don't!

I battled back and forth with my brain, which I believed was a separate entity from me. Like an evil twin that wouldn't leave me alone. I now felt guilty for falsely thinking I wanted my mom to die.

I would need to confess this to her later to undo the thought before it came true.

* * * * *

I would later learn these are called intrusive thoughts. The way I manage them now is to talk to a friend or family member and tell them I am having the thoughts. I can run whatever I am thinking by them and ask if it's true, or if it is a distorted thought. When I talk to someone I trust, they are almost always able to help me get through it. However, it is not always easy to maintain clarity and it may take me a while to achieve freedom from that thought. Talking to someone I trust usually makes it better and at least I feel less alone.

* * * * *

It had become so hard to keep track of all my confessions that I began to keep a little red notebook next to me to write them all down. I purposely wrote sloppily and in code so no one could read my secret shame.

Time came for a pop quiz in math. This one would be timed with ten minutes to complete twenty problems. I reasoned this would be no problem for a math whiz like me. As I wrote my answers, my mind told me I did not write down the correct answer. But my eyes were looking at the correct answer. My mind won this round and I erased and rewrote the same answer again. But then, maybe my eyes were seeing wrong so I needed to erase and rewrite again, this time paying closer attention. My paper started to rip from all the erasing. Time was running out and I still had fifteen problems to go. Thank goodness I am good at math and was able to answer and rewrite my paper several times before the teacher called time!

Then came lunch. Fellow students buzzed around the loft, their laughter and scraping chair legs hitting my ears like hammers. I scrunched my face up to try and block it out.

The cafeteria was even louder. I sat with girls from my violin class and ate my rectangle pizza as quickly as possible so I could head out to recess. *Ahhh*, the calm settled on my ears. I headed to my favorite spot under the oak trees to play on the big rocks, far from the bullies playing tag around the jungle gym.

After recess came my favorite class with my kind teacher, Mrs. Glen. She was young and new to our school and not aware of my past incidents which had established my reputation as a "bad" kid. I loved her feathery hair and soft, soothing voice like my mom's. She wrote on the top of my paper that I was imaginative, clever, and a special girl—complete with a smiley face. Mrs. Glen believed in me. She never gazed over me, but chose me to read my poems aloud to the class, telling them to pay attention to my use of imagery. Mrs. Glen helped me to believe in myself, if only for forty-five minutes. I wanted to hug her, but I just smiled and she smiled back.

I noticed teachers were starting to give me tests at school that they weren't giving to the other kids. On one occasion, the instructor showed me cards with words and I had to read them to her. I loved to read, so this was a piece of cake! At the end she told me I was reading up to a 12th grade level and I was in 4th grade.

Wow, I knew Mrs. Glen would be so proud of me. I felt accomplished, unlike how I felt in class when most teachers just looked over me. Now the teachers would have to believe I'm smart and maybe someday I would earn one of the awards or certificates they were always giving out. I really wanted one of those awards. I knew I was smart. I knew I was capable and creative. In some other people's eyes though, I was an inconvenience. I was just taking up space in the teacher's otherwise perfect classroom. I envisioned getting an award and walking onstage as my classmates applauded.

Dealing with my obsessions and rituals at school wasn't easy. I refused to use the bathroom at school. The blaring screech of the fire alarm terrified me. It occurred to me one day that the alarm could go off while I was going to the bathroom. I would be all alone and dazed by the piercing sound. Lost and confused, I would burn up in the fire. So, no bathroom breaks for me! Occasionally, I had accidents, but that seemed like a better option than death by incineration.

My mom wanted me to ride the bus home. Teachers hurried us to gather our things and line up. I made sure my red notebook was in my backpack. I am very organized and methodical, but I become easily distracted when rushed. Then I find it easy to forget things. I freeze during transitions, finding it hard to start a new trajectory.

Boarding the bus, I sat near the front—far from Tim, who sat in the back with the cool kids. My stop was the last one. I didn't really mind because I loved to stare out the window as we drove and unfocus my eyes. The colors of the world outside lulled me to a relaxed state after a day of tension.

Arriving home, I ran inside and hugged my mom. I did it! I kept her alive another day. After our happy reunion, I pulled out my red notebook. As she put away laundry, I trailed after her, confessing the day's intrusive thoughts.

CHAPTER 9

Starting to Ask for Help– What's Going On?

"My hand is laughing."

Starting in fourth grade, my right hand would become very weak and limp so I could not hold my pencil. I would say, "My hand is laughing," because it felt almost ticklish. It came on suddenly and I had no control over it or how long it lasted. To compensate, I would try to write with my left hand until it went away. One time a teacher questioned me about why I wasn't writing and all I could say was that my hand was laughing. The whole class giggled at this, but she wasn't amused and didn't understand. From then on I kept it to myself, afraid that no one else would ever understand.

By the age of ten, my mom and dad noticed that my differences were taking over my life. My mom took me for some testing at a nearby hospital. After a long day of different activities and answering questions, we drove home. As I grooved to "I Heard It through the Grapevine" while munching on my Smarties candy, I felt light inside, realizing that people were trying to help me. I later learned that I had been diagnosed with Sensory Processing Disorder, which I didn't really understand at the time, but confirmed there was a reason I hated loud noises and commotion. I felt a great sense of relief knowing that my extreme reactions were not a sign of me being a bad kid. Maybe now things would get better.

I would have outbursts in school where I would run out of class or the auditorium during assemblies to hide in the coat racks under all the bags and jackets. I did this to escape noise or misunderstandings with my teachers. Out of concern, my mom started coming in for meetings. Sometimes the school counselor would pull me out of class to talk. My mom also entered me into counseling outside of school, which I hated. I felt embarrassed that I had to go, and I did not want to let all of my secrets out. I was too ashamed of what I interpreted as my weirdness.

I remember the counselor would try to get me to talk about things that were going on with me, but I would just shrug my shoulders and say, "I don't know," as I had done many times before. It was so hard to articulate what I was feeling. If I did not understand my obsessive thoughts, how could she? I had a hard time looking at her and I just wanted to be done.

The one-on-one communication was too intense. It felt like I was being interrogated. Like with my principal, I just shut down. My mom was able to get things out of me more organically, but then out of shame and fear I would not tell her about the over-and-overs. I was actually afraid of the "men in the white coats" coming to take me away to an institution. That was a common expression in the 1980s and I took it literally.

One day, in my counselor's pile of games, I saw Hungry Hungry Hippos. I *loved* Hungry Hungry Hippos. My mom wouldn't buy it for me because she said it was a mindless game with no educational value. Maybe that's exactly why it appealed to me. And in all fairness, it did require strategy, using geometry and other math skills. The premise was simple: get all the marbles. Then you got to smack the lever repeatedly in a rhythmic frenzie that was ironically relaxing. My counselor used this to her advantage, and she said if I talked to her, we would play Hungry Hungry Hippos at the end. This mesmerizing game served as an incentive, but I still just gave her the bare minimum to be able to play the best game in the whole world! I still didn't give away my innermost secrets.

Looking back, I wish I had told her everything. I wish I could have put into words all of the suffering, the over-and-overs, the rituals, fears, tics, teasing, and teachers. I wanted to scream it all out, but it was stuck inside of me. Even my love of words could not help me express my anguish.

Maybe my counselor didn't have the skills she needed to get the words out of me or to teach me to talk.

Maybe saying all these aloud could have helped me.

Maybe talking could have prevented the horror that was coming.

CHAPTER 10

A Middle School Friend Story

"The friendship seemed to work because we had common interests."

The summer before fifth grade, a new family moved into my neighborhood. I decided to get on my bike and do a little investigating. I rode up and down the street, trying to get a glimpse of who was moving in and if they had any kids.

Then I spotted her: a tall girl with brown hair I'd never seen at school before. She looked older and so cool. She was talking to Carol. *No!* I was scared she wouldn't want to be my friend after Carol, my nemesis, filled her ears with lies about me. I waited for my moment. Finally, Carol rode off on her bike. This new girl looked friendly and kind, so I took a chance. I don't remember who made the first move, but we ended up talking. By the end of that summer day we had built the start of a friendship!

I was elated. My new friend, Cara, was fun. Maybe because she was one year older, she was a little more mature and didn't really care about my differences. Plus Cara liked to ride bikes and play catch like I did. Also, she did not own the game Clue. Her mom let us eat marshmallows out of the bag and drink Kool-Aid! I was having the best summer!

The friendship seemed to work because we had common interests. For some reason, I was happy to follow her lead. Was it because she was older? Did she generate trust? Whatever the reason, I did not resent her leadership.

We would swing on her swing set, seeing who could jump off the farthest. Then we would play Madonna's "True Blue" cassette in the backyard and make up dances. I mostly played air guitar with a badminton racket.

Sometimes Carol would join us, but at this point I didn't even care. Cara and I were doing too well together. While we were playing, my obsessions and rituals—my over-and-overs—left me alone a little more often. I stored my intrusive thoughts and obsessive urges in one half of my brain, while I had fun with the other half. How did I know to do that? I don't know, but it became a huge help. I would deal with the over-and-overs when I got home.

Life had become a battle between the joy in my heart I was born with, and the sadness of my newfound fears and obsessions. These over-and-overs were like thieves coming to rob me of my joy. The Bible explains in John 10:10 that "the thief comes only to steal and kill and destroy; I [Jesus] have come that they may have life, and have it to the full." So, calling on Jesus, I fought valiantly to preserve my God-given happiness. I was always trying to get back to that joy I once knew.

Cara and I were best friends from that summer before fifth grade until the end of eighth grade. We did everything together. We played on the same softball team and practiced fielding every day after school. As we matured, we started watching soap operas and listening to Bon Jovi. We scoured *Sixteen Magazine*. I even followed her lead to sign up as a junior camp counselor at a nearby day camp. That ended up being a bad idea. I had no idea how to deal with younger kids, and the head counselors kept writing me up for my underperformance. With all of my issues (that I didn't yet understand and hadn't yet identified), I was not equipped to be in that role.

No one attempted to guide or train me as to what to do, and I did not have enough social maturity to work on my own. I was mortified, yet a bit relieved when they called me into the office and demoted me to camper. It was ultra embarrassing. Everyone else my age was a counselor.

At least I still had my best friend, right?

A terrible shock came at the end of that summer. One afternoon I rode my bike down to Cara's house, and she met me in the driveway. Her stepdad, Terry, who I was always a little afraid of, was out there too with a Coors Light in his hand. Cara caught me off guard. She said she was sick of me following her everywhere and us doing everything together. She didn't want me to come over and didn't want to be friends anymore.

Her words were so shocking. I couldn't believe that she had just said those things. She had made her point, but I still kept asking why. Where did all this come from?

I could not process what was happening. How could my best friend just turn on me? I froze, standing in her driveway, holding my bike. I refused to leave, because this did not seem like reality. Her stepdad then told me I needed to go home. He raised his voice at me and snapped me out of my daze.

I was sick. Sick to my stomach. I felt a pain deep in my heart that I had never felt before. This was the pain of betrayal. I rode my bike home and ran inside, crying from way down deep in the pit of my stomach.

I was in agony. I was hurt and confused. I did not see that coming at all. It took my mom hours to drag out of me what was wrong. That was something she couldn't fix. She couldn't make anyone be my friend.

Looking back, I'm sure there were signs that Cara was growing apart from me. She was maturing much faster and perhaps I was—in her eyes—becoming an annoyance. Almost every middle school girl has lost a good friend, so my experience was not unique. What was unique was I had a lot of trouble reading people and situations. I typically felt confused by people's facial expressions and tone of voice. If she was giving me cues that she didn't want to spend time with me, I never picked up on them. I just didn't get it. Or Cara might have kept it all inside, not wanting to hurt me.

I had grown too dependent on Cara. Cara had become my world, and now I was lost.

* * * * *

I entered high school alone. I was traumatized, afraid to ever make another friend. I had acquaintances at school and on my field hockey team, but no one to hang out with.

I became very lonely and that led to depression.

I also started pulling my hair out in clumps. I didn't know why I felt this intense urge to start pulling one day. But here was another over-and-over that seemed to relieve tension inside of me, at least temporarily.

This obsession scared me because I could actually see the huge pile of hair building up next to me. But still I could not stop.

By this time I had given up on trying to fix myself and feel happy. I just pulled with abandon.

I no longer really cared about my academics. I only tried hard enough to get C's so I could stay on my field hockey team. That was the only activity that brought me relief from the sadness.

On top of this, I came home one day to find my mom in bed, and everyone standing around her. She had been diagnosed with cancer. My worst fears were coming true. My mom was dying.

I did not want to even be alive. I became numb. Just going through the motions of everyday living. I kept telling myself, "Well, I'll stay alive until field hockey is over. After that, who knows." The girls on my team were kind to me. I had been moved up to the JV/Varsity team because I was really good at taking penalty hits.

The older girls looked at me like a little sister. One day they invited me to a team dinner, and there was a piano at the house. I started playing a song I had written, and the girls were amazed. They told me, "You *have* to do the talent show!"

But I definitely was not feeling up to doing it. They kept on me, making me promise to sign up. Under pressure, I reluctantly agreed. Not being one to break promises, I signed up. On the night of the show, my brothers and dad were too busy to come and my mom was too sick. I had to find a ride there and I was really scared. The show was *long*, and I wasn't on until the second act.

The kids had become very restless and let's just say they were brutally honest. If you were boring or bad, they let you know. I was terrified. What if they made fun of me or yelled things out? But I had made a promise.

When the popular cheerleader who was emceeing announced my name, I walked across the stage to the piano with my head down. I sat on the bench, sweating. I started playing. As soon as I heard the music coming out of me, I relaxed. Playing music had that effect on me. I was able to move my body to the rhythm, and everything else—including all those kids in the

45

audience—disappeared. I played my song with all my heart. It started out in a minor key, sullen and timid, and then my song crescendoed into a bright, hopeful, major key. At that moment of the key change, the kids stood to their feet and started clapping and cheering.

For me.

For that minute they were in my world and they felt what I felt, and none of them were too cool to show it. I had broken the barrier. I felt amazing. I finished my song with a smile and took a quick bow before running off stage. My life may have been in a minor key up until then, but I knew in my heart that my key change would come...someday.

CHAPTER 11

My First Hospitalization– This Didn't Feel So Bad

"I felt like I was running laps around my own thoughts."

That talent show was exhilarating. I was accepted, respected, and cheered.

But that was the last thing I remember about high school. In November of tenth grade, the darkness returned. It oozed its way into every part of my being. I now understand that it was several life-changing traumas at once.

- My older siblings had grown up and moved out.

- My mom had cancer.

- Puberty was upon me, transforming both body and emotions.

Individually, these would have been challenging for any tenth grader to deal with, but all of them simultaneously, along with my undiagnosed autism, multiplied my inability to cope. To compound matters, I had no friends to help me process all this. After losing my friend Cara in middle school, I had briefly built a friendship with a girl who rode the bus with me. After school we played Nintendo and made funny videos with my dad's camcorder. But she got caught up with another crowd and I was again alone.

My brothers had grown up, moved out, and were living their own lives. I believed this didn't include me anymore, even though I knew they still loved me. My body was changing so quickly and I felt uncomfortable in my own skin. And though my mother survived cancer—and is alive to this day—I believed my biggest fear of my mom dying would become real.

As a result...

- Everything was dark. I could barely see the sun in the sky.
- I had grown weary.
- I could not focus anymore.
- I was starting to fail classes—even though my IQ qualified for Mensa status and I had made stellar grades before.
- The happy parts of my brain were drowning in fear.
- Overall, I was not well.

One Friday afternoon, my parents called me into their bedroom to talk. I was blindsided when they told me I was going to be admitted to a nearby psychiatric hospital. A few weeks earlier, my mom had taken me to the pediatrician, who asked me tons of questions. Now it made sense: my parents and doctor were concerned.

My parents were firm with me in this decision. Perhaps they knew my reaction might be severe. They said I would be admitted on Monday and that I did not have a choice in the matter.

All weekend I worried. I had never stayed away from home before. I was terrified with a hint of curiosity. So many thoughts tumbled through my head. How would I be able to keep my mom safe while I was away from her? How would I take a shower or use the bathroom? Who would do my bedtime ritual with me? Would they be able to help me? I packed my things and waited.

On Monday we drove about thirty minutes north to New Hampshire into a country town with rolling green hills. The hospital looked like a small, quaint version of the big facilities that I was used to seeing. It was only two or three stories high and the grounds were well kept. It looked inviting enough. We walked inside the sliding doors into a spacious lobby with plentiful couches. The woman at the desk seated us and instructed us to wait for someone to come get us. Meanwhile I took in the surroundings, trying to catch a hint of what was to come.

Next, another woman came along with a big guy named Bert. My parents signed a bunch of paperwork and talked to the woman as I sat there nervously. Bert had already grabbed my duffel bag, and when I tried to take it back he firmly stated that he would take care of it. This started me down the path to panic. Why was this stranger touching my things? I was new to this world, but that seemed suspicious.

After the paperwork, the woman and Bert took us up an elevator to the second floor. We arrived directly outside my assigned unit in between two heavy-duty doors. The doors were my second hint that something wasn't right. Bert took us into a small room to the side. He went over a list of rules with me and handed me a copy. I was so nervous at this point that I don't think I heard anything he said.

Then it was time to say goodbye. He rang a buzzer and the heavy door to the unit clicked and opened. We all stepped inside. The first thing I noticed was the smell. It didn't smell bad, just...sterile. The lighting was kind of dim and it certainly didn't look as fancy as the lobby. A few teenagers sat at some tables and they all looked up, watching me intently. I would later learn that a new patient was an exciting break from the monotony of the unit.

Bert walked behind the desk with my precious duffel bag and a nurse introduced herself. After this, everything happened so fast. They told me to say goodbye to my parents, and after hugging them repeatedly and trying to go through the goodbye ritual with my mom, the nurse urged my parents to just leave to "make it easier." When the heavy door closed behind them, I ran to open it. I wanted to go home! But to my shock and dismay, the door was locked. I could see my parents through the small, thick glass window in the door, and I started banging on it, yelling and crying. Reality had just hit me.

Bert came over to me and asked me to stop but I didn't. He then told me, "We can do this the easy way or the hard way." I had no idea what the hard way was, but I didn't want any part of it. I finally willed myself to stop banging.

As I continued to sob, a female nurse walked me back to my room. It was a really big, empty space with four beds, one in each corner, and a dresser next to each bed. My duffel bag was already on one of the beds. She opened it and started going through it. She was touching all of my things! Then she got to the picture of my dog Sara and me which I had packed. It was still inside the picture frame. She told me if I wanted the picture, she would have to take it out of the frame. In my mind this would destroy the picture, and I couldn't make a decision. In the end she took it out and just left the picture on my bed.

Next, she said I was going to be subjected to a body search.

No!!!

Like most young women, I was extremely shy about who saw my body. I wouldn't even change in front of the other girls in gym class, and this woman wanted me to get fully down to my underwear and search me! I just wanted this all to be over and to be left alone. I very slowly started taking off my clothes. She put on some gloves and searched through the pile of clothing. She then got a clipboard and looked over my body, making notes. It was mortifying but I was in such a state of shock that I just went through the motions of it. After that horrible search, I was finally left alone.

I sat on my bed and cried, hugging that picture of my dog Sara and me. I had never been more scared or alone. Eventually I fell asleep on top of the covers, with that picture stuck to my wet face.

In the morning I was feeling slightly less anxious. I joined the others for breakfast. As hospital food goes, I would give it a B+. Even better, though, were the teenagers' responses to me. This unit consisted of teens and adults. The other teens were welcoming to me. None of them teased me like the kids at my school. They were curious about me and sincerely seemed to want to get to know me. I wondered if this was because they were all going through a hard time like me. I started to feel comfortable around them.

On the unit we would have groups where we were supposed to talk about our feelings. This led to awkward moments of silence as we teenagers sat with our arms crossed and our eyes rolled. We were determined to show the counselors we couldn't be cracked that easily.

Once each standoff was over, we would play cards or Rummikub for hours, joking and telling stories. Not only were the meals tasty but we even got to order what we wanted like we were in a restaurant. I was excited to try bacon, since I wasn't allowed to eat pork at home for religious reasons. I acclimated well to the strict routine, and was making friends along the way. However, it wasn't all rosy.

My obsessions and rituals were still in full swing, and my newest fear was catching AIDS. This was in the early '90's and even though I was old enough to understand how it was transmitted, the illogical part of my brain convinced me that I would catch it from the toilet seat or even someone breathing near me.

Since I was in an environment where I had to share a bathroom and other spaces with strangers, this fear came to the forefront. To keep myself safe, I started washing my hands every time I felt like I had been exposed. I performed this ritual so much that over the next few days my hands started to crack and bleed. The nurses noticed this and, without my knowledge, were taking notes about my behavior.

One day, my doctor asked me about my hands. I looked down at my cracked and bleeding skin. I broke down. Sitting in this empty, sterile room across from this stranger, I felt like I was in a whole other world. Even though I didn't know him, he had asked the right question at the right time. What *about* my hands? What had I done to myself? I could finally see at least one of my problems with my own eyes.

Although he was a stranger, it all came out of me. All of the years of "I don't know" were done. I felt like he wouldn't judge me. I told him all of my secrets. About the over-and-overs, the doors, the locks, the erasing, the notebooks, the goodbyes, all of my worries and fears. I was crying with snot running down my face but I didn't care. My confession went on and on. When I finally stopped to take a breath, he gently explained to me that these were symptoms of Obsessive Compulsive Disorder. This was something that was real and had a name. It wasn't just me being ridiculous, and it wasn't my fault.

As I processed this information, I started to feel relief, as if the entire world was lifting off my shoulders. At least for the moment. He explained to me that he was going to give me some medication that was supposed to help, and I believed I was going to be cured.

As the sun set after dinner, medication time was announced. This was uncharted territory for me. I had feelings of both fear and hope pumping through my heart. As I peeked into my little cup, there were more pills than I expected. The nurse informed me of the possibility of extreme side effects, and that if I felt any of the symptoms she described that I needed to tell her immediately. This terrified me.

About thirty minutes after taking my medicine, I started to feel very strange. I felt really heavy in my chair. Time felt slow and my body felt numb. My mind was running so slowly and I felt like I was running laps around my own thoughts. I was trying to latch on to anything real, like that dust in the living room years ago. I didn't know it at the time, but I was given heavy-duty anti-psychotic medications. Soon my whole world would become a blur for many years to come.

CHAPTER 12

The Next Hospitals–
Comforting Routines

"Institutionalization...home no longer felt like my home."

Despite the eerie medication side effects, I grew accustomed to hospital life. Oddly, I felt more comfortable and safe there. At the hospital there was a routine, and other teens to play games with. I perceived (though sometimes falsely) the staff was there to make sure I was safe.

I loved the rules. I had a bedtime and a wake-up time. I knew when to eat and what would be offered since we received a menu slip to fill out every day. I know now that my new comfort in this place is called institutionalization—an unintended consequence—and it happened so fast. Even though I felt the hospital was a better place for me, ten days after I was admitted my time there ended.

When I got home, I was terrified of the freedom I had. I felt alone again, and my old fears resurfaced. With no staff checking on me during the night, I felt afraid again of devil hands grabbing me, fires, or bad men breaking in. The lack of routine at home caused my anxiety to increase. I didn't know what to do with myself, so I turned to music to soothe me.

One day, I began playing the piano in the living room until my dad started yelling from upstairs. He was speaking out of his own fear and anguish about my mom's illness, but I didn't know that. He screamed, "Don't you know your mom's dying and you're down there making all that noise?!"

My heart sank because he had never spoken to me that way before. He always *loved* my music. In an unhealthy response to my father's beratement, I banged down on the piano keys. This caused my brother to get involved. He was less than patient. Tensions were high in the house and we got into a fight. My brother ended up restraining me. I felt like everything had changed since I was gone. I felt like I no longer knew my family. Home did not feel like my home. I was heartbroken and my family members were too.

After that incident, my family readmitted me to the hospital and so the cycle began:

- I would stay about two weeks in a hospital due to insurance limits on length of stay.

- I would be discharged home.

- The transition and change in routine would be too much.

- My behavior would spiral out of control, which frightened me and my family.

- I would get readmitted to another hospital.

- No matter how well or poorly I was doing, I would get discharged back home every time.

I don't know if it was the medications, the fear of my mom's illness, or the fact I was more comfortable at the hospital, but I couldn't function at home anymore. Fear over my mom's illness was a typical, and caring, reaction. I got frustrated—the same frustrations that would bother any teenager—but I didn't have the tools to manage the frustrations. Instead, I was hurting myself and being destructive. I wonder now how things could have been different if the hospital personnel had taught me coping skills rather than just medicating me. Life at any of these psychiatric hospitals has its own subculture, and I had to learn and adapt to each one. Also, the honeymoon period for me was over. Some staff were kind and respectful; others seemed to assert their position of power to belittle me and the other patients. I would frequently get in trouble for being rambunctious—jumping or climbing inside to release tension, repeating words loudly, and refusing to go to bed were just a few of the things I got punished for. Punishment usually meant losing outside "fresh air" time. This small punishment would lead me to hit my head out of frustration and I would be punished further with seclusion, or even restrained.

Why didn't they teach me, rather than just punish me? Why didn't they show me how to manage tension or frustration?

CHAPTER 13

More Hospitals–Ever-Worsening Horrors

"I needed him to not be a terrible person."

Restraints were barbaric. I was often restrained using a four-point restraint—where my wrists and ankles were locked into cuffs at each corner of a stripped-down bed. It was inhumane and I felt like an animal. I was placed facedown on a bare plastic mattress, so any sweat or tears smeared onto my face and body, burning and giving me cold chills. The cuffs were always so tight that my hands would throb and go numb. Since I was facedown, I had to keep turning my head left and right because laying on one side for too long hurt my neck. If I had to go to the bathroom, I was out of luck. I either had to go in a bedpan that they brought or pee on myself. I never could use the bedpan with the staff looking, plus it was difficult because I was laying on my stomach.

Between the position they tied me in and the side effects from my medicines, it was hard for me to pee. I always ended up just going on myself. I would then be even more wet and cold and they would leave me in there, like that, for hours. Sometimes all night. When they would restrain me, they would also give me a shot of strong medication like Thorazine and Benadryl to "calm me down." Mostly, they just wanted to keep me quiet.

Then one horrible night, I was almost silenced forever.

I had been admitted, yet again, to the psych unit at a local hospital. I was very upset about something that I can't remember. The staff wrestled me back into four-point restraints—except this time they placed me on my back instead of on my stomach. This frightened me more than usual because

I felt extra vulnerable and exposed to anyone who might walk by. I was crying loudly when suddenly, a male nurse came into the room. He grabbed a pillow that was under my head and put it over my face. He pushed down and was smothering me, screaming, "Shut up b----!"

At that moment, I truly believed I was going to die. He was going to kill me. I couldn't breathe. He *was* killing me. I tried desperately to take a breath but my oxygen supply was cut off as the pillow filled my mouth and nose. I prayed to God for help and that if I did die to please take me to heaven.

As I was crying out to God another staff member walked by the little room, possibly because they heard him yell, scream, and curse. This staff member flung open the door, screaming at the male nurse, "Are you crazy? Stop!"

The offending nurse yanked the pillow off me and walked out of the room as if he had not just attempted murder. I gasped and took a deep breath. I received no apologies. Instead, the staff kept me in those restraints well into the night.

The next morning I immediately called my parents, barely able to articulate anything because I was so traumatized. All I could do was repeat, "He's going to kill me."

Thankfully, they heard the true desperation in my voice and they came right away to see me. When they arrived, I was still unable to describe the incident, rocking back and forth and repeating words to soothe myself.

They recognized it was serious. Eventually I got the story out, and the department for protection was called. They interviewed the staff member who had intervened, and he admitted to everything he saw the offending coworker do to me.

Then my dad had me immediately discharged and my parents took me home. I was told that the offending nurse would never be allowed to work in a facility again. That's it. No charges. No apology. No restitution. Nothing.

He should have been criminally charged with assault.

But he wasn't.

None of them ever were.

The staff that got caught abusing us never faced consequences besides being moved to a new unit or possibly getting fired, only to get hired at a new facility.

CHAPTER 14

Residential School Mismatch–
Nowhere Else to Go

*"These were mostly geared toward...runaways or...other
risky behaviors. My very different situation...was an
autistic brain that would not function typically."*

In between hospital stays, I frequently got discharged to residential schools. This happened because living at home had become too difficult for both my family and for me. I didn't want to take my medications because they made me sleepy. I argued with my mom about this, who I'm convinced agreed that she didn't like what the medicines did to me. Also the lack of routine at home made me feel off-balance and scared all the time, as if something bad was going to happen around every corner. In the hospital at least I knew what was coming.

The residential schools weren't a good match for me. These were mostly geared toward girls who were runaways or chose other risky behaviors. My very different situation—still not diagnosed—was an autistic brain that did not function typically. At every new place, I had to try to read people and assess situations very quickly, as we were given little to no introductions or time to process. Due to my autism, I had *a lot* of trouble decoding people's mannerisms and social cues. I felt thrown to the wolves.

Another indication these residential schools were not the best places for me was that no amount of talk therapy was going to help me. We did a LOT of talking. I never knew what to say. I hated it. I felt like the leaders were fishing for dramatic stories of a terrible childhood or abuse in my family. I had neither of those experiences. My family was supportive and caring.

What I needed were strategies for my over-and-overs, coping strategies for my obsessions, and actions that would improve my social skills. These things were nowhere on their radar.

I was constantly having meltdowns from the noise and other environmental stimulation. My meltdowns were treated as intentional outbursts. They were not. I wanted to control them but I couldn't. During a meltdown, my body would energize and tense. For a few moments I would be very still, and then I would burst. I would throw myself violently into walls or pick up and throw the nearest objects. Sometimes I would drop to the floor and be unable mentally to make my body get back up. This terrified me. I would have done anything to get them to stop.

But the staff did not believe this. The staff tried to force me to stand up, which led me to different kinds of self-harm.

I also picked up a new behavior at these schools. I watched the other girls self-harm by cutting themselves with razors or any sharp items they could find. It was the cool thing to do, so I tried it. It became a cycle that became hard to break. I am not proud of it because that choice was voluntary, unlike other behaviors I had no control over. It was something I did out of peer pressure, to fit in, and to get attention.

* * * * *

I don't self-harm anymore because now I know how to get attention the right way. People outside these residential schools taught me more effective ways to relate. These days, if I need attention from my staff, I will tell them what I need. For example, I might say that I'm lonely and so I want to talk or interact. I learned to just be honest and open rather than try to manipulate the situation by cutting myself. I think that's part of growing up, being more mature, and learning that not everything is going to revolve around me. But I would not have gotten here without people to help me.

* * * * *

Eventually I was sent to a locked, intensive, residential school, located in a wooded area down a long, dirt road. As soon as I arrived through the double-locked doors I sensed the tension in the air. An overly stiff therapist with a perfectly permed mullet greeted me. As usual, I had trouble reading her facial expressions. But I did have the ability to feel the emotional temperature in a place. I sensed danger in her seriousness. Sadly, I was right.

After my brief orientation, I was left to navigate this new world on my own. Jessie was the first girl to talk to me and she was surprisingly chipper. She invited me over to her doorway during free time. She chatted up a storm. Even though her intensity overwhelmed me, I decided I should feel happy to be making a friend on my first day.

Then her stories turned strange. She began telling me that when she first got there she didn't change her underwear for weeks until the staff made her. Well, that was some information I didn't ask for! One thing I noticed about these facilities was whoever spoke to me first was usually the person with the most outlandish background story. Jessie didn't disappoint.

The girls in that facility all seemed to have extreme personalities. They constantly fought for attention from the staff. This created a huge problem: If one girl did something dangerous or destructive, other girls would try to do something worse. I felt unsafe in this chaos. My obsessions worsened as I used them to try to create order in that tumultuous world.

We weren't allowed to say certain words as they were triggers for other girls. I constantly worried I would utter one of these words by accident. We couldn't play cards because that was a trigger for one girl in particular. We couldn't watch most movies or TV shows. I didn't understand this at all and so my fears got worse, believing there was something magical about all of these restrictions.

They also had this crazy rule about pens. We were all assigned a pen, and if we lost it, we received a major punishment. The reason was that pen and fork swallowing seemed to be all the rage. I didn't even know that was possible! How do you swallow a fork? I was interested in the details (not that I had a craving for silverware or writing utensils). My roommate confirmed this was a real thing, and that she had recently swallowed three AAA batteries.

I was astounded. My mind was trying to visualize how one would do this, and an even bigger question was, "Why?" She told me this would get them a trip to the hospital, which was the ultimate goal for most of the girls. They craved attention, no matter the personal cost.

Eventually I settled into this strange world, but I refused to embrace the culture. There was rarely any laughing allowed. Why not? Isn't laughing healthy? We were all afraid to talk because every subject or word seemed to be taboo. Doesn't talking things out solve the problem? Rather than help me, the situation was stifling. I hid my joy deep inside so it wouldn't be stolen by that place and those people.

CHAPTER 15

Friendship in the Middle

"I still wonder what they were trying to teach
us. What outcome did they expect?"

Punishments outweighed the offenses in the hospitals and residential homes. Or they simply didn't make sense. For example, it was a major crime to "move conversation away from the staff" by talking to a peer without direct supervision. On a regular basis, I would get timeouts and have to sit on the couch in the hallway or at the desk under the stairs. I most often got sent under the stairs because apparently the couch was "too rewarding" for me.

These frequent timeouts were unfit punishments for me. Time passed unbearably slowly and I could not sit still for a whole 15 minutes without some kind of sensory input. I needed to be moving, working, or mentally stimulated in some way. So I would find ways to entertain my mind. I would rock back and forth, repeat words, tap rhythms on the desk, or sing. Instead of the staff or therapists helping me, they would assign more punishments. Eventually they gave the major consequence of being sent to the seclusion room for hours on end. The hours I spent being punished were hours wasted, when I could have been learning what I actually needed: social skills, academics, and self-regulating techniques.

I still wonder what they were trying to teach us with those punishments. What outcome did they expect?

A few times I was restrained in something called the safety coat, which the girls had nicknamed 'the human burrito.' It was a long piece of canvas that had straps and buckles attached. We were placed inside, lying down with arms at our sides and wrapped tightly with the straps. Even though I typically liked the feeling of pressure and small spaces, the human burrito made me feel like I was suffocating in a coffin. Also, it was easy to overheat inside there.

After this punishment, I still had time to serve on my sentence. I had to do a major chore restitution, like cleaning the nasty shower drains or washing a huge pile of pots and pans. After each restitution, staff members led a meeting where the offender confessed what she had done wrong and how she would improve her behavior. Then the community got to vote by raising their hands on whether to accept the offender back into the group. This lengthy process could take two or three days. We held these feedback meetings every day at 3pm. They were actually kind of entertaining if you weren't the one on probation. We always voted people back into the group because we didn't want to be on the receiving end of a downvote when it was our bad day.

During one of these meetings I met my kindred spirit, Sandi. I had known her name but had never talked to her. She was popular with the staff and residents, well-liked, and well-behaved. Those characteristics appealed to me in this place of chaos. The girl on trial that day was being funny by doing a hilarious voice impression of her teddy bear, but we weren't allowed to ever laugh. While trying to hold in my laughter I happened to catch eyes with Sandi, who was also stifling her amusement. We smiled knowingly at each other. Everyone else was staying serious but we couldn't hold it any longer and both started cracking up. Unamused, the staff sent us both to timeout on the couch in the hall. We then started talking to each other, making more jokes. That's when I got relocated to my spot under the stairs, but I didn't care. I had begun a new friendship.

To quote from the movie *Forrest Gump*, Sandi and I were like peas and carrots, meaning we were well matched, better together, and got along well. We spent free time together daily and developed a way to speak in code so we could be silly and make jokes without the staff picking up on it. Man, was Sandi funny! She entertained me with hilarious stories about her family and teachers growing up, while imitating their voices and facial expressions. While we talked we drew dozens of pictures in crayon, each one having a hidden meaning of an inside joke. The jokes were based on events that went on in that place. We would giggle as the staff hung our masterpieces on the wall, unaware that each one was a story in itself. Everyone there was so serious and didn't see the humor in our bizarre little world. I was so glad I had my Sandi.

* * * * *

why are you crying
why is your heart black and blue
friend tell me your story
what have they done to you

don't suffer alone
share your worries and fears
I'm here for you love let your light shine again

don't cry any longer
i'm here and together we're stronger
hold my hand pick you up
off the ground

hold your head up high
let the stars in your eyes
your future is bright
don't let the past hold you down

i'm right by your side
and i've been through the dark clouds
of doubt
so walk with me
and we'll find our way out.

* * * * *

Sandi naturally understood me. And I understood her. She was empathetic to my obsessions and fears; I tried to show care for hers as well. When we talked about our lives, we discovered we felt the same way about most things. She could finish my sentences and thoughts as if we were twins. Sandi knew me so well that when I would have my moments of inconsolability, the staff would get her to come and talk me down. She knew exactly what to say to "fix" an obsessive thought or help me break out of a ritual. She saw what I needed and was able to effectively help. We learned that even though we had different lives growing up, somehow we were brought together in this place. We did not believe our meeting was by chance, but instead a gift from God.

The epitome of our schemes happened at dinner one summer night. Somehow, Sandi and I were assigned to the same dinner table. Typically the staff kept us apart because they had deemed us "overly silly." Dinner was always simple and usually not very appetizing. That night was hamburgers and curly fries. I picked up a bun to make my burger and it was so stale that it was rock hard. I nudged Sandi and clanked it against my plate. There was no way we were eating that, so we decided to have some fun. I grabbed two curly fries, dipped them in mayonnaise, and stuck them on the bun to look like eyes. We chuckled. The supervisor, unamused, gave us a timeout warning for playing with our food. We tried to settle down but it was too late. Sandi's eyes lit up and she grabbed a straight piece of curly fry and dipped the end in ketchup, placing it between the top and bottom bun as a cigarette. She said, "Look, it's a happy burger!" in her authentic Boston accent. She then made it talk to me like a puppet. I fell out of my chair laughing. The supervisor, with her "resting mean face," was done with us. "That's it!" she said. "Both of you have timeouts."

Sandi was sent to the couch and I, of course, was sent under the stairs. From my spot, hidden out of sight, I let out a snicker. Sandi heard me and giggled. Soon we were belly laughing again. That's when our supervisor did something unprecedented. She sent us to our rooms upstairs! She barked, "Get upstairs...I don't want to see you talking, laughing, or even looking at each other for the rest of the night! If that happens...heads will roll!"

When she said, "Heads will roll," we lost it. Her overreaction was just making things worse. We ran upstairs, where all the other staff were laughing as well. One of them had even saved our masterpiece from the table and was showing it around. Happy Burger had broken down the wall between all of us. If only for one night, we were joyful and felt just a little bit free.

* * * * *

Sandi and I eventually left that program within weeks of each other. It turns out we had grown up not far from one another and we stayed best friends. I was really happy for her that she got to go home. The world needed Sandi. She would come visit me in whatever facility I was in and we would laugh so much our faces hurt. Kindred spirits. Being with her just felt easy, like we had known each other for every day of our lives. I'm convinced kindness was the reason. She cared and showed it.

Sandi doesn't have autism, but she took the time to understand me, and to figure out how to help me. She was like my coach back then. Sandi is also an overcomer who is strong. She is oh-so-smart and quick-witted. I truly admire her.

I remember one time we went ice skating. There were some teenagers pointing and laughing at me, making me feel like an outcast. I was the only brown face in a sea of white faces. Between that, my autistic habits, and the fact that I was very overweight at that time, I knew they were laughing at me. I was not imagining it.

I grew hotter and hotter inside, warm tears streaming down my cold face. I skated off the rink and then I melted down. I was screaming and throwing anything near me. The manager told us to leave and that he was calling the police. I ran outside into the cold night and just kept running. I wound up in an empty office park. Sandi had chased after me. When I realized it was just us, I cried from the pit of my stomach as she hugged me tight. When I had calmed down, we headed back to the car but the police were there! Sandi promised to protect me. As we approached them, she explained what had happened because I was still without words. Amazingly, some Good

Samaritans, who had seen the kids taunting me, took my side and told the police I was being bullied. They let me go home with Sandi.

These days, Sandi and I live far apart and don't get to see each other much. But when we do, we pick up right where we left off as if no time had passed. Now that's a friend.

* * * * *

I learned from Sandi that just because I spent time with someone, that didn't make her or him a friend. Real friends are people who:

* *have a mutual relationship, balancing the give-and-take*

* *will not use me or let me use them*

* *laugh with me and not at me*

* *bring out the best in me and let me do the same for them*

* *talk me down or calm me down and let me do that for them*

CHAPTER 16

Group Homes–Good Ones were Rare and Bad Ones were Terrifying

"Nothing was safe including my money...and even myself."

Even Sandi couldn't fix institutional madness.

Once I aged out of the school system at twenty-two, I started to live in group homes. My first group home was remarkable. The staff cared about us and tried to teach us new skills so we could become more independent. They played games with us and took us out to concerts and fairs. We had a menu and helped cook every day. I loved it there and started to grow as a person.

But after only a few months, the company that ran the group home decided to drop our home, and another company picked us up. That's when things got bad.

Once the new company took over, I started getting my things stolen, even by the staff. Nothing was safe including my money, my necklace that my brother had given me, my CDs, and even myself.

The house became filthy.

We stopped learning life skills or doing community outings and instead were left to sit in the house and entertain ourselves. Quite understandably, I had trouble connecting with the new staff. I felt incredibly alone and unsafe. I was accurate in my assessment. I WAS unsafe there.

We often ran out of food by the end of the week and had to eat cereal for every meal. We had a food budget but the staff didn't keep up with making menus so the food would get used up too quickly. We residents were often left to fend for ourselves for meals so we just ate whatever we could find, including junk food. One of the spare rooms had a mattress propped up against the wall. I used to go in there and pull the mattress down on top of me in an attempt to soothe myself. Once my caseworker found out about this new habit, she arranged for me to go to a sensory center, to see if that could help me. I liked going to the center a couple times a week. I worked on regulating my senses—especially touch, movement, and body awareness. These three were the hardest for me. The sensory center gave me a weighted blanket, which I loved.

Still my autism remained undiagnosed.

The sensory actions helped tremendously. But overall, and unfortunately, this help came too late. I had grown severely depressed and I could barely get out of bed. Was it any wonder with the conditions I was living in that I didn't want to leave my bedroom? Then I began hearing voices that weren't there, whispering to me. I urinated in containers so I wouldn't have to come out of my room as often. The staff had to force me to get up and go to my day program. The day program consisted of hanging out and drinking coffee. Sometimes we had group classes about job skills or we had paperwork to do, but mostly it was a place to keep us occupied until the staff arrived at our group home. The new company didn't staff our house during the weekdays.

My apartment-mate, Chuck, became obsessed with stealing my CDs. I tried locking them up but he would break the locks. The staff were no help. They didn't care. They stole my stuff too. One day when I got home from my day program, Chuck was playing my Third Eye Blind CD loudly in his room, purposely, so that I would hear he had taken it. He then came out, taunting me by lip syncing the song "Semi-Charmed Life" right up in my face. He realized nobody would help me. The staff did nothing to stop his behavior or protect my things.

I snapped. I swung and hit him. Then I broke open the medication box and took a whole bubble sheet of pills.

Everything had been building up to this point. Even without autism these conditions would have been unbearable. I decided to make the pain stop. The frustrations, the loneliness, the dirty—both physically and socially—environment...I couldn't stop them, so I just wanted to disappear.

The staff called the police. When the officer arrived, they encouraged him to arrest me. But there was something in this kind officer's heart that stopped him. He recognized my last name. He said he had known my brothers growing up, and that they were good guys. He stated firmly, "No, I'm not taking her...she doesn't belong in jail."

That police officer saved my life. If he had locked me up, I would have died from an overdose. The officer saw the white residue from the pills on my lips and questioned me about it. I admitted I had taken pills, so he called an ambulance instead of taking me to jail.

By the time I got to the hospital, I was starting to fade. I didn't realize it at first, but I was wheeled into the room where they take people who are dying. They stuck a tube directly down my throat. The nurse implored me not to go to sleep and rubbed her knuckles on my sternum. This hurts tremendously when you are fully conscious. I didn't even feel it. The light started to fade from the outside of my vision until I could only see a little tunnel in front of me. I knew then that I was in trouble. I was dying and I felt alone. I felt nothing but emptiness. There was no bright light, no kind voice calling to me, nothing.

I prayed, "God, don't let me die." I just kept praying. That's the last thing I remember before waking up in the ICU the next day. I was alive. I was relieved. I would love to say this was the point at which my life turned around...but the treatment I endured would only continue to get worse.

CHAPTER 17

Skin Shock and Applied Behavior Analysis–Legalized Abuse

"I WANTED to do well, to get well. But nobody helped me."

No group home or other outside facility was then willing to admit me into their program due to my intense behavior. I admit my behavior had become extreme. But what they refused to look at was the cause. The places and the staff were dooming me to failure. My autism was still undiagnosed so I received no help for it (except that wonderful weighted blanket).

As an adolescent I had been placed in homes with girls whose behaviors included swallowing things, cutting, and running away. Those homes didn't match my needs. Then as an adult I was sent to group homes where I was overmedicated—leading to severe weight gain, sleepiness, and depression. People were controlling me externally with drugs rather than teaching me internal control. I WANTED to do well, to get well. But nobody helped me.

At the first sign of me having a meltdown the staff would immediately call the police. They gave me no help, no life skills, no intervention.

* * * * *

Although my behavior was a clear cry for help, it all culminated in my being committed to the state hospital—indefinitely. In the state hospital, I was placed on a permanent room program, which is a euphemism for seclusion. My program stated I had to sit on the floor of the empty, cold seclusion room for fifty-five minutes of every hour. For the last five minutes, I was allowed out to use the bathroom or sit in the dayroom. Then, at the top of the hour, I was returned to my cell. If I verbally refused to comply, I would be put into four-point restraints, even if I wasn't out of control. The only thing I was allowed to have for entertainment was a deck of cards (which was always missing some cards).

This treatment not only did nothing to treat my undiagnosed autism, but was incredibly dehumanizing. Rather than identify their actions as the mistreatment it was, I turned the feelings in on myself: I think because I couldn't understand facial expressions, I would get even more mixed up. This resulted in me crying or yelling when I thought anyone was looking at me. I concluded they were looking at me in a bad way or whispering about me. I felt I had no purpose for living. I had no one to talk to. Most of the other patients were so sick that they couldn't interact. And the staff hated me.

* * * * *

The staff interpreted my responses (which in hindsight were very healthy responses to cruelty) as me being overly sensitive or self-centered. They retaliated. They treated me coldly and refused to meet my needs. It wasn't right, and it wasn't my fault. But it's just what they did. This made me hate myself even more. Some staff would even taunt me and arrange for the other patients to hit me. I didn't feel like a human anymore. I had literally become a punching bag.

As most people would expect, I got worse and worse. I needed to get out of that room and out of the meaningless life I was living. Like in residential schools, the lack of mental stimulation or input was hard on me. It would have been hard for anybody.

I was so drugged I believed I would simply not wake up one day. I weighed almost 300 pounds due to the large doses of Depakote. They used this strong seizure medication as a mood stabilizer. But I had no seizure disorder or mood instabilities. I had autism.

When the social worker came to my mom and me with news of a possible new program that was willing to take me, we were elated. They made it sound like Disney World. I would live in a big, beautiful house in a regular neighborhood and go on trips to the community. Maybe it would be like that first group home! According to the social worker, the school had its own arcade and weekly field day that was like a carnival. I was very excited. I would do anything to get out of my current place. I thought it was going to be great!

My mom and I were hopeful. So a few weeks later the social worker, one of the state hospital's doctors, and I went to visit the new place located south of Boston. When we arrived, staff members led us into a beautiful room that was decorated in a Disney theme. When I say decorated I mean it was over the top. I had never seen anything like it. Big Mickey statues, a bright colorful rug, fancy chairs, and wall art. The place looked incredible!

But something wasn't right. After introductions, a woman came to take us on a tour. One thing I noticed about her was that she never really smiled, even as she showed us the reward center. I didn't tell anyone my hesitations. I even talked myself out of them.

The reward room looked like a real arcade with large video game machines, a popcorn machine, twinkle lights, and couches. Again, it *looked* incredible. Kids were playing games, listening to music, and eating snacks. Our tour guide got us some popcorn and a drink out of the soda machine. I remember getting a Fruitopia.

But something about the place was empty.

And they didn't show us all the rooms.

* * * * *

their college papers, license to decide my fate

their eyes watched me tense with the jolt

cold and still they studied my torment

notes on a paper,

just another day

* * * * *

We continued the tour around the upstairs of the building, poking our heads into classrooms filled with apparently contented teenagers. The boys were all wearing shirts and ties, and the girls were also dressed up. What teenagers do that? They were all sitting at desks facing the wall and working on their computers in silence, tapping—what I would later learn was mindlessly—on their keyboards.

Then I noticed the kids didn't even look up when we interrupted. This didn't make sense to me. Typical kids would look up and be curious, even act a bit mischievous. But these teens weren't acting like you would expect from a classroom full of kids.

I started to feel a little anxious. Something felt dangerous about this place.

But because I was so desperate to get out of that state hospital, I again pushed my worries to the side.

After the tour, the program's administrators went to talk privately with my social worker and the doctor. Another staff member took me for a walk. Little did I know, my social worker and doctor were discussing the truth about this new program and what it would mean for me. I should have known that excluding me from my own treatment meeting was suspicious. But I was used to being left out of them.

Meanwhile, the staff member took me down the stairs. Woah! This was no ordinary staircase. It was decorated in all sorts of old fashioned Coca-Cola merchandise—clocks, paintings, and 3D wall hangings. The old Coca-Cola theme song playing *on repeat*. It was creepy.

How I wish I had listened to my hesitations.

When we got downstairs and rounded the corner, I spotted an old friend of mine named Mike who I knew from previous group homes and hospitals. Mike was the most unique person I had ever met. He was very small for a grown man, and he was extremely determined at getting things he wanted, like a cigarette or a sip of alcohol. He was also very energetic and really didn't care what other people thought. Mike was very special to me because we had been through a lot of things together at our other placements and although we argued a lot, we understood each other deeply and had endured scary times together. Mike had a way of getting into your heart, and never letting go. I admired his strength despite his size. I respected his determination.

Mike was sitting on a metal butterfly-shaped bench next to a staff member when he saw me. He yelled out my name, "Jennifer...hey Jennifer!"

The staff said something to him to try to quiet him.

But he continued yelling, "Jennifer...don't let them send you here! They will shock you. Don't let them send you here, Jennifer!"

This time the staff grabbed him by his thin arm and escorted him roughly back down the hallway. I asked the staff member who was walking with me what Mike was referring to but she just brushed me off.

Now I really should have started paying attention.

Soon the social worker, doctor, and I were on our way back to the state hospital. The sun was setting over the city skyline as we drove north through Boston. I let my eyes unfocus as I stared out the window and relaxed my brain. Mike's words were ringing like alarm bells in my mind. Suddenly I remembered! At our old group home, one of the staff had explained to me that Mike used to get electric shocks at his old placement. I didn't know what she meant back then, and I had no reference for what a shock entailed. I figured it was like when you walk with socks on a rug. Right? Or was it? Wait, were they going to do that to *me*? If they did, how much could it possibly hurt?

A little bit of my Fruitopia came back up into my throat.

* * * * *

When I arrived I wasn't scared,

but the air told me something different

It was heavy,

try as they did to paint it pretty

Music played, colors danced on walls, but the air...

All too soon new reality was upon me,

wires tracing skin,

snakes ready to strike at the push of a button

It's not OK to misbehave and you surely will be punished

Do not speak and do not cry,

Do not scream,

You'll soon know why

* * * * *

The day came for me to be admitted into the new program. I was so excited to leave the cruel hospital that I persisted in ignoring the warnings about where I was going. I didn't even complain when the ambulance drivers put my hands into restraints for the transport. I was out of there!

Upon arrival, a whole group of staff were waiting by the main door. *Why so many?* I wondered. They let me off the stretcher and rapidly escorted me into a small room. A large bald man introduced himself as my case manager and went right to business, having me sign paperwork. I was twenty-five years old at the time, and technically my own guardian. I did not understand what he was making me sign, but I just did it.

* * * * *

I didn't know it at the time, but during my admission they also made my mom sign paperwork saying she would not pursue guardianship over me. She was trying to save my life and thought I was going to a wonderful place. The danger was well-hidden from anyone who could help me, including my mom. My advice to families, particularly if your family member is non-verbal, is to research every facility thoroughly. Do not depend on tours alone. Ask to see every room. Request the names of families whose children have graduated from the program. Ask for three positives and three negatives from these families and from anyone you talk with. Find and review official records. Ask to see specific treatment plans. Your family member's health— and maybe life—depends on it.

* * * * *

My case manager then quickly went over my new "treatment" program, which was just a long list of categorized behaviors I was not allowed to do. It included the strangest forbidden things, like "shaving eyebrows, failure to follow dress code, and high-fiving other students." *What did that have to do with right or wrong?* I thought. There were so many rules on this paper that there was no way I could remember them all. A few others I could remember were "no running through buildings, no speaking to students on LOP (loss of privilege)." It was too much to process.

The case manager then took me down the elevator into my classroom. No Coca-Cola stairway this time. More warning bells went off in my head.

The "classroom" was the furthest thing from a classroom because the walls and floor were covered in red safety mats. There were two students being restrained when we walked in. The other staff and kids were stepping over them as they walked in and out of the room. The reality of what was in front of me was certainly not going to be my fate. Or was it?

I was told to sit at a table, facing the wall. The 1:1 staff assigned to me threw about five washcloths down on the table and told me coldly, "Fold the towels, please."

"What?" I asked.

"No talking out," the staff barked back.

Wait, what was going on? I was just trying to clarify the instructions. I did not understand what they wanted from me. Why were they asking me to fold towels that had already been folded until the staff threw them down in front of me? I didn't know what to do except to sit there with a blank stare. The staff then prompted me by saying these terribly confusing words:

"Work on your task, please."

More blank staring from me.

"Not following a direction to work on your task; work on your task, please."

"There is no not following directions, break your multi-day contract, break your less-than-a-day contract!"

"What?" I said. (Are you confused by this language? Because I sure was.)

"No talking out, you're on LOP (loss of privilege)," said the staff.

I then tried to raise my hand to get the head staff member's attention, but he just commanded me to put my hand down and work on my task. He said he would talk to me when I was "back on contract."

I began to feel like I was in a movie. Was this some sort of bizarro world where everyone knew what was happening but me? I was like a foreigner in a land where I didn't speak the language. I had only been in this new place for an hour. I started shaking uncontrollably. No one would answer my questions. They just kept yelling at me to fold those stupid towels.

* * * * *

What I didn't realize was that I was in a program that used Applied Behavior Analysis (ABA) to "treat" behavior issues. ABA uses rewards and consequences in an attempt to alter a person's behavior. I am not an expert on how it's supposed to work, but I'm almost 100% certain this placement did not use it correctly. Wouldn't behaviors like thoughtfully articulating feelings and organizing my day to get both work and play completed be the right behaviors to reward? Why teach me to fold towels when I could do that like a champ? I don't know why they did that, but I do know what I suffered through because of it.

* * * * *

Out of frustration that none of my attempts to communicate were respected, I grabbed the towels and threw them on the floor. As soon as they left my hand, I was snatched out of my chair and thrown to the mat on the floor. The staff wrestled me into a giant, smelly safety coat made of canvas and leather. This one looked like a man's hunting coat, but the end of the arms were sewn shut and then covered with extra layers of canvas and leather. Being inside one is horrible—and doesn't feel safe in any sense of the word. The coat was incredibly hot, it smelled, and it made me feel like I was suffocating. Not only was I forced inside the coat, but the staff also laid on top of me with all their weight, forcing my face into the dirty mat. This sitting on top of me while I was restrained went on for approximately thirty minutes before they finally started to let me sit up. I was in a daze. I sat back at the table and quietly folded my towels.

Later that night, around 7pm, we got ready to board the buses to our assigned houses. I was relieved to get out of that red room. I joined the other seven residents who were in the red room. Staff members placed us in transport restraints, which locked around our waists and had locking cuffs for our wrists. Then there were shackles for our ankles and another restraint that pulled our arms down even further called a "crossover." I felt like a prisoner, but I was ready to leave that "classroom" at any cost.

A staff member escorted me onto the bus and sat me near the front. Almost immediately, the two girls sitting behind me started giggling and thrusting their knees into the back of my seat. I turned around and they started calling me names. I started to cry. I tried to ask for help from the staff member, but she just yelled at me, "No talking during transport, break your transport contract." The girls laughed even more and started kicking the back of my seat even harder. This hurt me both physically *and* emotionally. I continued to cry the whole way to my new residence.

* * * * *

Asking for help was wise and right. These staff members were charged with helping me, with taking care of me. But I learned in both this placement and previous ones that I couldn't always trust staff members to help me. One thing I learned over and over was that asking for help could get me into worse messes. This made me take matters into my own hands, which put me into even more danger.

* * * * *

The next morning, staff members put me back in restraints and when I got on the bus, the girls started to tease me again. But that day I was not taking it. I started yelling and thrashing around, trying to get off the bus. Staff members held me down in the seat, and then I was removed from the bus. *Good*, I thought. Then they brought me onto a white van they called the "safety van." It had one seat in the middle with about twenty different straps and restraints attached to it. It looked like something used to transport the most dangerous of prisoners. They strapped me in so tight to the seat I couldn't move at all. They also stuck a red karate helmet on my head. Then off to school.

I wish I could say that my second day was better, but things only got worse. When I got to my red mat classroom and sat down, out of nowhere I felt a heavy object strike me in the head really hard. The impact was so severe I got dizzy. What had happened to stun me like that? When the stars cleared out of my eyes, I saw one of the other girls laughing and shaking a full soda bottle. She started threatening me, and I lunged for her, determined to defend myself this time. We were both taken down to the mats by staff members. She continued to threaten me. It turns out she wanted the 1:1 staff who was assigned to me and my existence put a wrench in her plan.

After that incident I was moved to a room covered in blue mats. The teacher seemed more understanding and made me feel more relaxed, but my relief only lasted a few minutes. At that point, I was no longer allowed to sit at the table because I kept throwing my towel-folding task around, which was the only thing I was allowed to do. Now I was made to sit on a hard plastic restraint board in the middle of the classroom floor. I had to sit there from 9am until 7pm when we left the school. I had nothing to lean my back against and I would get restrained if I tried to lay down, so I sat, hunched over in pain all day. I was given other students' textbooks to read to myself as my task, which served no purpose, so I just sat there and stared at one page to avoid the staff yelling incessantly in my ears, "Jennifer, there is no stopping work!"

I was restrained a lot during this time, purely out of frustration from the pain of sitting like that all day. My new program stated that I would be strapped on to that restraint board if I didn't comply or even tried to stand up or get off of the board.

But why?

I realize now that I was being set up to fail on purpose. I was being set up to "exhibit behaviors" so that the program would have enough documentation to convince the court to put me on the shocks. Yes, my friend Mike had been right...they were going to shock me.

CHAPTER 18

A Rigged System–Skin Shock and ABA

"I would have done anything to get off the board.
Since I had never seen a kid shocked, I had no reason yet to be afraid."

Two months after arriving, a man introducing himself as my lawyer came to see me. He pulled up a chair next to my board where I sat, and he asked me if I knew what the shock devices were.

I told him that I had seen some kids wearing backpacks.

He said, "Yes the backpacks, that's correct."

I still didn't really know what they were. I had never seen them in use.

He then asked me if I wanted to get up off that board and sit at the tables again. Of course I did. So he told me I needed to go on the backpack program to do that.

So I agreed. Hardly informed consent.

I would have done anything to get off the board. Since I had never seen a kid shocked, I had no reason yet to be afraid.

One morning I was sitting on my board, and a bunch of staff members came into my classroom. They told me to stand up and started putting on all of the transport restraints. I asked them where we were going, but all they would say was, "No talking out," and ironically, "No not minding your own business." That made me laugh because it was so ridiculous.

Of course it was my business.

Then they said, "No laughing at inappropriate times," and I just felt sad. Were these people robots? Was I on an alternate earth in another dimension?

They then strapped me into the safety van, and off we went. The ride was long, especially since I had no idea where they were taking me. We got caught in traffic because there was a terrible accident on the highway. I knew someone had died. I could feel the heaviness in the air.

We finally pulled into a huge parking lot, and I saw a courthouse in front of us. Things were starting to make a little sense. The lawyer, then the courthouse. When they got me out of the van, I realized another student had followed us. He was ecstatic to be there. He kept saying he was excited to see Judge Judy, which made me chuckle and helped lighten the mood. I don't think he grasped that this was very wrong.

They made us go into the court building with all of the restraints and red helmets on. That was embarrassing. They ushered us into the courtroom where things went *very* fast. My "lawyer" was there, and some other lawyers representing the facility. They told the judge about all of my "dangerous and aggressive" behavior, showing him charts and graphs of all my incidents.

Mind you, standing up off of that board was considered an "aggressive behavior," so the picture they painted was definitely not fair. My not doing the ridiculous tasks like folding the same five towels repeatedly was considered a non-compliance—another major behavior.

My numerous restraints were mostly caused by the painful position I was made to sit in for ten hours a day. Every time I would try to change position or lay down to stretch my back, I was tackled and placed into restraint.

I had been purposely set up to fail. I was not the only one this happened to. This gave the lawyers a set of fake evidence to have an open-and-shut case with the judge.

The lawyer worked to convince the judge I was a serious danger to myself and others. But the danger actually came from others. I was the one in danger.

I did not get a chance to speak in court and it was over as quickly as it started. We began the long van ride back to the school.

As soon as we entered my classroom, all the other kids were ushered out. There was my board laying on the floor. A bunch of staff members were there as well as my new case manager, Helen. She had been in this position for a couple of weeks already but never had really spoken to me. Now she was there speaking kindly to me, which was odd.

* * * * *

*I feel it is **really** important for parents/friends of people in these facilities to really make their presence known to the staff. Make surprise visits and phone calls, and don't accept that you are not allowed to talk to your loved one at a certain time because of their "behavior." This might be the most important time you need to talk to them to find out about any mistreatment going on. If your family member or friend is non-verbal it is really important to stop by for visits often, if possible. If they live far away, insist on video chatting with them on a regular basis. If there is a rule against this, be very wary.*

* * * * *

Usually staff members spoke to me with a cold voice, so as not to "reward" me with kindness. Helen asked me nicely to sit on the board, and as soon as I did the staff jumped into action, restraining me.

They placed a backpack on the floor next to me. There were holes cut into the bottom of the pack, with wires coming out. These wires were covered in a thick white canvas material about two inches wide. At the ends of these wires was hard, clear plastic, six inches long and two inches wide. On the underside of the plastic were two silver metal disks. These were the electrodes that provided the shock, as I was soon to find out.

The plastic parts also had locks attached to them, with straps to wrap around the arms and legs and to lock the electrodes into place.

Five of these wire sets came out of the bag. They looked like snakes to me, even though I did not yet know how they would bite me.

On the other end of the wire sets and inside the backpack were hard plastic boxes with batteries into which the wires plugged. The backpack was to hold all five of these heavy batteries.

I had a sinking feeling.

The staff went to work attaching these wires to my body. I remember the personal invasion of their hands, feeding wires down my pant legs and up my shirt. They even locked one of those wires around my bare stomach. It all happened so fast. I felt more than violated.

When the staff finished their macabre routine they released me from the board and told me to sit up. They instructed me to put the backpack on. I was still traumatized, so I followed their directions blindly.

The backpack was massively *heavy*. The weight of it pulled my shoulders down and it was hard to breathe. Then, as if putting the cherry on top of a sick sundae, sweet-talking Helen took one of those locking straps and weaved it through my backpack on my chest, effectively locking the bag to my body. She patted the lock with a satisfied smile and seemed very pleased with herself.

"Call me if anything happens," she said in a singsong voice, leaving the room.

Other staff members then instructed me to go sit in a chair at the table, something I had been craving for weeks. I eagerly sat down. Then the nurse came in with my medication. They were in the process of weaning me off medicines, but I was so intent on being med-free, I usually refused to take them at all.

As usual, I told the nurse I didn't want the medicines. Instead of walking out of the room, she went over to my staff member and looked over my program sheet with her. This was the list of all things for which I received consequences. My staff member picked up a clear plastic box with my picture on it that she had hanging on her apron. She opened the velcro closure which made a very distinct sound, and pressed one of the remote buttons inside. Fire ripped through my calf muscle as I heard a high-pitched whistle coming from my backpack. My entire left leg involuntarily shot out and lifted off the ground. I lost my breath and time stood still.

After the eternity that was actually two seconds, the ripping, pulling, burning feeling subsided into tingles, and my leg relaxed. The staff then stated coldly, "Jennifer, there is no refusing your medication."

I sat there, out of breath and confused. Then the staff member told me to turn back around and work on my task. Those darn washcloths again. Only this time, my mind was blank with shock. The conditioning of my mind had begun. They had my attention and I did as they asked.

Later that night at the residence where I lived, I got another shock for "getting out of my seat without permission." I had stood up from my bed to use the bathroom.

Reality still hadn't set in.

As the days went by, I was weaned off the safety van and had a seat back on the regular bus. The girls had stopped teasing me by now, and were starting to be kind to me. Looking back I realize they pitied me, as they knew from experience what I was in for.

Falsely kind Helen, my case manager, came to see me often and look over my behavior sheet. Soon she moved me into a regular classroom, without mats, where I had my own desk and could work on real work and use a pencil. That felt better as I was treated more like a person in that classroom. I was also starting to learn what I wasn't allowed to do. I had rewards that I could earn if I passed certain behavioral contracts. For example, if I did not have any HDB (health dangerous behaviors) for 24 hours I would be eligible to go to the big arcade upstairs to play games and eat popcorn. If I *did* have HDB, I would suffer consequences including electric shocks and be placed on LOP (loss of privilege).

Being on LOP was horrifying for me because, while on LOP, staff would purposely treat us meanly, nobody was allowed to speak to us, and we were not allowed to speak unless it was a work-related or medical issue. Also, while on LOP you had to sit at your desk all day from 9am-7pm doing work.

The contract I hated the most was the one that said I could not have a phone call to my mom unless I managed three days without any major behaviors and with fewer than ten minor behaviors. Minor behaviors included rocking or verbal repeating, things I couldn't help doing because of my autism. I still had my tics, which were getting worse because I was coming off of medications. This made me want to move a lot and wiggle and wave my hands and try to get that energy out. But all of this was considered a "behavior."

The staff would stand right behind me and bark in my ear:

"Jennifer, there is no handplay."

"Jennifer, there are no non-functional body movements."

"Jennifer, work on your task, please."

"Jennifer, no not working on your task. Work on your task please."

The entire process was disorienting and unspeakably cruel. Staff would bark directions at me so fast that I couldn't follow them, causing me severe frustration and anxiety. Any sane human would feel that frustration and anguish.

Then I would just explode.

I would jump out of my seat and hit my head with my hands. Then they would shock me for self-harm.

This became a cycle. I almost wanted it to happen to get it over with. Lest you think I was destructive (I wasn't), what I mean was they had trained me to know the pain was coming, and I just wanted to do the bad thing to get it over with so I didn't have to worry about it happening. This came from my obsessive thinking.

I would also instinctively try to grab the box of buttons on the staff's apron to protect myself. I wanted them to stop shocking me. It was human nature to try and protect myself from pain.

Soon I was labeled as aggressive because of this. In reality, the staff members were the aggressive ones. They even modified my program so that if they decided I showed any aggression or self-harm, I would be placed on the four-point board and be given five shocks over a period of ten minutes (instead of one shock immediately).

This was an even more terrifying consequence because I would be locked, helpless, on that board and shocked multiple times, never knowing when shocks were coming. It was a horrifying game of anticipation.

What kind of sick person thought this torture up?

I got nauseous when my case manager explained this new consequence. I was trembling and couldn't eat for days. I knew it was just a matter of time before I received this five-shock consequence.

* * * * *

Somehow it's OK to hurt those who are a little more different.
Somehow it's easy to turn the other way.
If one can't speak to express it, of course they still feel pain
and the sadness of knowing that it is not OK.

Doctors, judges, papers in hand
buttons and wires, backpacks and plans
shocks and screams,
begging you to stop.
Crying, "No more!"
Knowing it's not
The locks on your wrists, ankles and head.
The mind wanting safety has already fled.
Turn back around, do as they say;
Follow directions, you might be ok.
Heart beating wildly, sweat sneaking in.
Wires just waiting to bite at your skin

Stomach in tangles, heart black and blue.

Doctor how would you feel if this happened to you?

* * * * *

The day came. Or night, rather.

I had gone to bed and I still had a one-to-one staff member who stood in my room to watch me. My program said I had to keep my hands over the covers and my staff members had to be able to see my face. This made it hard to sleep because staff members would keep waking me up, directing me to uncover my hands and head. Also, I had to sleep with the lights fully on. Added to that, a motion alarm system would beep loudly every time someone moved in any room on the hallway. On top of this, I had always had a hard time falling asleep since I was a kid.

This particular staff member seemed to love the power of her job. She stood in my room, talking loudly to the staff member across the hallway, disregarding the fact I was trying to sleep. I could not fall asleep with her talking, but she kept giving me directions to go to sleep.

Finally I said, "How am I supposed to sleep when you are talking? You are making it impossible for me to sleep." She did not like me challenging her. She started reading my behavior sheet, trying to find something she could shock me for. Between the frustration, sleep deprivation, and fearful anticipation, I lost it. Death seemed safer than this constant torture. I leapt out of my bed and flung myself at the wall. I banged my head and it went clear through the wall several times. Then I jumped to the window and put my head through the glass several times. I wanted to break through and fall to the ground and die. Staff came running and wrestled me down.

As I slowed down, I realized that since I wasn't dead, I was in *so much trouble.* I saw the night supervisors whispering. Then they shocked me twice for destruction of property. That was it. Done. They sent me back to bed.

I didn't realize it at the time, but they did not want to be the ones to give me the consequence I really had coming.

CHAPTER 19

From Horror to Terror–Skin Shock and ABA Got Worse

"Sunlight refused to pour in as if the day knew to be respectful of my impending doom."

The next morning, I felt a sense of relief after sleeping. But I also felt dread. I knew my case manager was not going to be happy and that I would now be on LOP (loss of privilege) status, probably for a while. (Looking back, LOP is sadly comical. What privileges did I have, really?)

When I arrived at my classroom, which was now the adult workshop, my supervisor got a call telling her not to take me out of my transport restraints that I wore every day to and from the school. My stomach sank. I asked the supervisor what was happening, but she couldn't even look at me. I knew that meant it was very, very bad. I tried not to throw up. I trembled with fear.

My staff then told me to stand up because I was going to get my batteries changed on my devices. This was a typical thing they did every couple of days; I had to get put on the four-point board where they took all the batteries out and put fresh ones in my backpack. As if I were some sort of inanimate object, like a car. I hated it, but as it was one of the less painful treatments, I was used to it.

I knew though, that today this was a lie. They weren't interested in changing my batteries. I walked with them down the hall slowly, as if I was walking to my death. *Dead Jen walking!* I thought to myself with some sort of dark humor, trying to keep the dread from taking over. My stomach was sick and my body cold. I tried to muster up strength and bravery for whatever pain lay ahead.

We entered an empty classroom where there lay a four-point board in the middle. Nothing else. Even with the blinds wide open, sunlight refused to pour in as if the day knew to be respectful of my impending doom. I didn't fight even though I knew something beyond terror was coming. I became very calm and matter-of-fact. This was going to be bad. This was going to hurt but I wasn't going to let them see my fear. I was not going to give them the satisfaction of knowing my terror.

After they strapped me down, a case manager named Cheryl came into the room. I remember staring at her chunky-heeled shoes as she paced around me. *Click, click, click* they went as she looked everywhere but at me, lying strapped down, helpless on the floor. She had my behavior recording sheet and the device that held the remote buttons to my electrodes. I was terrified, waiting for the first shock, not knowing where it would hit me: leg, arm, or, worst of all, my stomach.

The anticipation of pain was part of this particular punishment. Shocks were given at random intervals for the specific purpose that the student victim didn't know when it was coming. These actions created absolute physical and psychological torture. There are no other words for it.

I followed her with my eyes, looking for any indication that the first shock was coming. But she was good at this. I was not her first victim.

Suddenly, shock number one came. The high-pitched noise of the device screamed out, but I didn't. Even though I wanted to scream, it was the one thing I could control, to not give her the satisfaction. I steadied my breathing and I kept watching her, trying to get a clue as to the timing of the next shock so that I could prepare my mind and body. The trick to not screaming was to keep my muscles slightly stiff and relax the rest of my body, taking deep breaths. Shocks two and three came, and now sweat and tears were pouring off my face. My clothes were soaked.

I would not scream in pain, so I absorbed it and held it deep inside where you bury your worst experiences. I placed it somewhere else to be dealt with when it was safe. Never here, never now. I could not let her know my fear. Shocks three and four came and I didn't feel my body anymore. I was floating. I urinated on myself and I didn't care. I could have died and it wouldn't have mattered. My heart was beating so fast and I asked God to make it stop so I wouldn't feel shock five.

Five came and went, but still she did not stop. My consequence was supposed to be five shocks. Why wasn't she stopping? Even more panic set in as I realized she had changed the rules. When would she stop? Then shock six came. Cheryl continued to pace, clicking her shoes on the floor as if she was the most important person in the world. She looked at her watch every so often. I resolved myself to my fate. I told myself to concentrate on absorbing the pain and hide it inside of me. No matter how this went, I wasn't going to give her satisfaction.

Thirty minutes and ten shocks later, it was over. Another staff member came in to change my batteries, as if integrity mattered to them. Then I was taken back to my workshop. One part of me felt weightless, relieved it was over and that I had survived. But every other part of my body hurt. My muscles had tensed involuntarily during the shocks and now ached. Circular scabs had formed where the electrodes had attached to my skin and burned it. I was stiff and in pain.

* * * * *

If you are wondering why or how anyone could ever work at a place like this, it appeared that at least some of the staff had been convinced by the administration that they were truly helping save our lives. I could see several of them felt conflicted between their conscience and what they were ordered to do. The staff who were empathetic eased up on us when we were outside or somewhere not under the surveillance of the cameras. Others justified their cruel actions because they needed a paycheck. They looked the other way from the atrocities happening in front of them. Then there were the ones who loved the power they were given over us. Maybe they had no power in any other part of their lives. They loved administering the electric shocks. Off camera they were nasty. They laughed and relished in our suffering. I would have to learn how to survive these things. All three categories of staff perpetuated evil. Even the ones convinced that they were helping knew deep down that their actions were wrong.

* * * * *

The other students had heard what had happened and consequently communicated a feeling of reverence in the room. They whispered to me, asking if I was okay. That expressed care was like an unspoken rule. When another student got shocked, especially on the board, the rest of us showed empathy to that mistreated one. We were all suffering this together, silenced by our captors, tortured in the name of treatment.

My freedom was incrementally stolen from me. Rather than help me, they had taken control of every physical aspect of my life. My body and my actions were no longer mine. They had also hijacked my mind in their attempt to rewrite who I was. Right off the bat, I realized they wanted to control how I thought and force me to comply with their program. They sought to make me a robotic version of myself. For the most part, they were succeeding because I was compliant to some extent.

Fortunately, I had my dad's stubbornness and I consciously decided to never let them have my God-given spirit. I vowed early on that I would never let them destroy who I was born to be. I protected my heart and my natural joy. I was sad and I was captive, but I sheltered my spirit. I did this by instinctively splitting myself into two versions of Jennifer. One was colder and dealt with surviving stoically. The other Jennifer held the most tender parts of my heart and soul. She kept me from being corrupted. At times they broke me, but that was their burden to bear. I went through the motions on the outside while I buried Jennifer inside my bones until the day she was free to shine. They had the upper hand, but they would not win.

* * * * *

Months into my "program," I was brought into a small conference room by my case manager. Sitting there were two administrators and a man I did not recognize. The mystery man was wearing an ill-fitting brown suit and his tie was fat and crooked. I was told he was my new guardian. He introduced himself and held out his hand, but I was already so conditioned to avoid physical contact that I just stared at him. My case manager told me I was very rude and directed me to shake his hand. Non-compliance was a shockable offense, so I shook his hand reluctantly.

How hypocritical, I thought. They won't allow me any physical contact unless it makes them look bad. Then they call me rude when I follow their rule.

The conversation turned to business. They talked about me as if I wasn't even there, going over paperwork—from court, I suppose. My guardian then started speaking about "the mother."

He said, "The mother is a problem."

I sat up. *Whoa, buddy.* He was entering sensitive territory. He then carried on about how my mother constantly "interfered" in my past treatment, and that she was a bad mother.

I got red hot inside. Who did he think he was? And since when was an involved mother a bad mother? Any study will show that the foundation to life success is a parent who keeps in touch and shows interest. In addition, this "guardian" had never even *met* my mother. My mom *protected* me. She had protected me from strong-armed art teachers and psychotic nurses who tried to smother me with pillows! She had literally saved my life! I wanted to reach across the table and strangle him.

But I stayed calm instead. I came to realize they thought they would be 'found out' by a perceptive mother.

He then insisted that I agree with what he was saying. I did the only thing I could figure to do without yanking him up by his tie. I sat silent and refused to look at him.

I mentally checked out from the rest of this meeting. When it was over, my case manager grabbed my arm roughly and escorted me out. She whispered coldly in my ear that I was very rude and non-compliant. Non-compliance was just her word for not letting them get away with the cruelty they imposed.

I could feel her hot-angry breath on my face. Then I felt a too-familiar searing pain in my arm. She shocked me for being non-compliant and for refusing to speak badly about my mom. I will take that consequence any day.

* * * * *

This institution's form of ABA (Applied Behavior Analysis) conse-quences and rewards created a new problem. I would try so hard not to do the certain behaviors I got shocked for, that I developed new coping strategies which were also considered shock-worthy.

For example, since I could no longer cover my ears or eyes to block out the over-stimulating environment (a shockable offense), I started a new pattern they called verbal repeating. I would repeat words or phrases to help block out noise and keep my focus away from the ruckus around me. The adult workshop I was in was overly chaotic, so I started this habit. By repeating words, I was able to focus inwardly on those sounds instead of the chaotic noises I could not control.

One day shortly after I arrived at the workshop, my case manager swooped in my classroom, all business. She had a brand new lunch bag for me as well. *This can't be good,* I thought. She pulled out a new bright-white behavior sheet.

"New program!" she said excitedly. "From now on, if you have five IVB (inappropriate verbal behaviors) within one hour, you will receive a shock. Then, for every single IVB after that in that same hour, you will receive another shock."

These were my actual IVB behaviors:

- arguing with staff members/students
- interrupting others
- nagging

- talking out (who determined what was conversation and what was talking out?)
- asking non-academic questions during academic time
- speaking in an inappropriate tone of voice
- making rude comments
- laughing/singing/crying at inappropriate times
- bizarre speech
- commenting about hearing voices
- seeing things
- nonsense noises
- verbal repeating
- talking to myself

I had been pinpointed for these behaviors constantly. Instead, I felt set up. I felt that way because I actually *was* set up. I wasn't doing these behaviors because they were inappropriate; it was nearly impossible for me *not* to do these things or to be accused of them, because of both my autism and my fear of shocks. Although my living situation would be considered cruel to any person, as a person with autism I had a lot of sensory issues that made it even worse.

That adult workshop was a sensory nightmare, with over 40 of us bundling popsicle sticks while staff constantly yelled and pinpointed behaviors on all of us. Add on top of that the shuffling sound of thousands of popsicle sticks and a heaviness of wood dust in the air and I found it unbearable to my senses. Day in and day out, this was my life.

On top of the list above, my case manager added, "Refuse to acknowledge staff within five seconds" as a shockable offense. Staff members were always calling me out for repeating or talking to myself, using an inappropriate (in their opinion) tone of voice, and nagging (asking to go to the bathroom more than once was nagging).

So if I answered their questions, I would be in trouble. If I stayed quiet, I would be in trouble. I was darned-if-I-do-and-darned-if-I-don't.

My case manager wasn't done explaining my new program. She added that if I did any of these behaviors, even one IVB or EdSoc (educationally and socially inappropriate) behavior, I would lose a portion of my meal.

My actual EdSoc behaviors were:

- non-performance of tasks (who defines *tasks* and how meaningful were those tasks? Remember folding the washcloths someone threw on the table?)

- stopping work

- mimicking others

- rude gestures

- rocking without appropriate stimulus

- avoiding eye contact

- manipulating objects

- facial grimacing, repetitive blinking

- pacing

- taking shoes off without permission

- blowing bubbles with saliva

- writing bizarre letter and notes

- handplay

How many of these are related to autism?

And once again, all of these behaviors were left up to the staff member to determine. Few of the staff (if any) wanted the best for me. Not only would I receive painful shocks, but now I would lose nourishment. I was reduced to earning my meals.

For example, my breakfast was cut up into little cups, like those salad dressing cups you get at restaurants. I only earned a couple bites of my breakfast every hour. No longer would I ever feel full at this facility.

I had to earn the right not to starve. Looking back, I can hardly believe this was legal, let alone moral. But it was all approved by the court and my court-appointed "guardian" (who was in cahoots with my "program"). My case manager's lunch box was for all my meal portions. I was not allowed to eat full meals anymore but I had to go to the cafeteria anyway and sit and watch the other students eat.

This did not go well. The hungrier I got, the more my body moved without my permission, and the more portions of food I lost. Being hungry, causing my blood sugar to drop, caused me to tremble physically and also caused my mind to become confused and panicky. I already had tics and urges to move my arms and legs constantly, and being hungry made it impossible to control these movements.

This went on for months until the entire institution was placed on a vegan diet. Nobody, including me, wanted to eat the new food. Eating was no longer a reward because I would refuse to eat my portions of seaweed. Mercifully, my persistence and stubbornness won again. I got off of that awful program.

For about a year, I was not allowed to take a normal shower because I was considered "too dangerous" to come out of my shock devices. Instead I was bathed on that same type of four-point board from the blue room. The facility had one of these boards in the upstairs bathroom. A female staff member would put me on that dreaded board, take all my clothes off, and basically sponge-bathe me. It was traumatizing and embarrassing. Having people touch me when I had no clothes on, and being strapped onto a board where I could not protect myself had me rightly feeling attacked.

I was completely vulnerable, powerless, and exposed. During every bath I would cry quietly the entire time. Things happened that I cannot even talk about in this book because I just can't think about it.

Once I was finally permitted to take showers, I still had restrictions such as one of my arms being placed into a restraint locked outside of the shower. They did this to keep one electrode on me at all times in case I had a "behavior."

I always put "behavior" in quotes because the actions they considered inappropriate, disruptive, or harmful were typically harmless. I also got shocked for tensing my body or even just my hands, and for "tic-like" body movements. I suffered from actual tics that I could not control but they punished me for them anyway.

CHAPTER 20

No Way to Win

*"This program was designed to keep us there,
exhibiting 'behaviors' so we could never leave."*

How was I supposed to improve and move up in my program if they kept adding things to the list of things I got in trouble for? If I was doing too well for too long, my psychologist would start making my rules harder to follow and my consequences longer. For example, if I went thirty days without a major behavior (which was rare) my psychologist and case manager would add more "behaviors" I would be punished for. They also increased the time it would take for me to be off of LOP if I did have a behavior. How's that for backwards logic?

Eventually I realized this program was designed to keep us there, to keep us "exhibiting behaviors" so we could never leave. This terrified me. I started to look around at students who had been there for years, their hair going gray, the life in their eyes dulling with ever-dwindling hope.

I could not let this be me.

* * * * *

This horribly tragic place that seemed to have no redeemable qualities actually *did* have one: the diversity. Many girls I lived with were Black or Hispanic. Finally, I did not feel like an outcast because of my brown skin. The days of coloring my hands with white chalk to cover my dark skin were now far behind me. As I watched these women, I wondered where they had grown their confidence in who they were.

These women and I encouraged each other. They raved about what beautiful curly hair I had. They showed me how to get my curls to shine. They affirmed it was okay for my hair to be fluffy and wild.

This mutual care was something I had not experienced in my life until this point. These women were a community and welcomed me into it. They didn't see me for my autism or reject me for my skin color. It felt nice to fit in and to be complimented on a part of me that I had foolishly learned to hate.

I did not have this acceptance by my peers growing up, but better late than never. I carry that confidence to this day. Also, now that I had been taken off of the heavy doses of medication from the state hospital, I rapidly lost my excess weight. Consequently, I was physically healthier.

But even the peer acceptance and my nice curly hair did not outweigh the torture of the shock treatments. Adding to the atrocities, the shock devices we wore malfunctioned. They would spontaneously start shocking without staff even pressing the button. Staff members would have to rip open my backpack and start disconnecting batteries. They called this a "misapplication." But it happened to me several times. Once we got caught in the rain during field day and my batteries got wet. After we came inside to the workshop, the device just shocked me for no reason. This phenomenon was especially scary because I had no idea if and when it was going to happen again. Just imagine how difficult sleep became.

One night after the staff had finished their routine search of the house for contraband, a staff member claimed she found a piece of sharp plastic in my self-care kit. This kit contained our hygiene items like shampoo bottles and toothpaste. Of course pieces of plastic broke off sometimes. I had a sinking feeling again that they were going to call this "possession of potential weapons." I was told to go to bed but I was apprehensive because I was afraid they were going to shock me. They assured me the matter was resolved.

I went to sleep and as I was just drifting into REM, I was jolted awake by a familiar pain in my calf muscle and a command, "Jennifer, there is no possession of potential weapons."

I woke up, terrified and confused as I sputtered and repeated myself, asking "What did I do? What did I do?"

The staff shocked me again for "loud repetitive talking out." Then they directed me to be quiet because I was waking up other people. *After they had just woken me up by shocking me!*

* * * * *

Sometimes the hypocrisy of the staff made me red hot inside. I felt like I was trapped in some weird cult but hadn't been brainwashed yet. After that night, I couldn't sleep steadily through any night. To help with this, and because I wasn't being monitored as closely by this point, I started to sneakily unplug the batteries in my bag every night. I would have gotten in a lot of trouble if I had been caught, but I had to take a chance because it was the only way I could sleep.

During the day, my main job was to bundle popsicle sticks for a food service company. It was called piece work, and we only got paid a penny per bundle (called a piece). I soon figured out I wasn't getting paid for my efforts, but the supervisor was averaging the number of bundles and paying us all the same no matter how much work we did. For example, if I did a hundred bundles and my neighbor did five, we would get paid the same. Besides being a mindless job, I lost all motivation to work because I wasn't getting paid fairly for my work. Some days I refused to work, especially if I was already on LOP.

I can think of no good result of this mindless work for any of the residents.

The staff would get mad because they didn't want me to think I could just sit there. So they would bark directions at me to start bundling twelve sticks. They were directing me so fast I could not keep up. No human could. And if I did not comply on time, they shocked me.

I started grabbing sticks and couldn't count them fast enough. The supervisor then directed me to bundle the *correct* twelve sticks. I couldn't count them as fast as she spoke, and I miscounted. Then she shocked me.

It was like a medieval sweatshop. I snapped, and I took the box of loose sticks and threw them across the room. Of course I was shocked again for that outburst but it felt good to rebel. It was the feeling of taking back any portion of basic human power.

This kind of ABA is abusive and doesn't truly help or change a person. As soon as the staff takes away the shocks or consequences, all the old behaviors come flooding back. Also, at least with me, it caused me to become even more obsessed with my rewards, since they were now nearly impossible to obtain.

To degrade the process even more, rewards became basic human rights—something as simple as food, a phone call to a loved one, or positive attention. These basic human rights now had to be earned.

Staff members even exploited my relationship with my mom, and they used her as a prize. They knew that's how they could get to me. I had to earn my own mother.

How could that be right by any definition?

CHAPTER 21

Family Connections Must Be Earned

"The program fought hard to keep my mom from reinstating her rights as my guardian, and the years kept passing."

Why didn't my family stop all this from happening? The answer is twofold:

1. They didn't know at first.

2. Once they knew, they were *trying*.

All of my phone calls home were strictly monitored and if I mentioned anything about the shocks or made complaints about my program I was made to hang up. My mom did not get the full scope of what was happening until I earned my first unsupervised visit with her. I remember sitting in the car, trying to tell her everything. The only time we had was to the ice cream store and back. There was so much to tell and it was so bizarre, how could she understand?

The more I went on visits the more I could tell my mom, but because she was not my legal guardian (remember the facility forced her to give up those rights) she could not have me removed. The program fought hard to keep her from reinstating her rights as my guardian, and the years kept passing.

* * * * *

This is the only type of ABA I have experienced so I will only speak to my history with it. A person's family needs to closely monitor the treatment their loved ones are receiving to know what's really happening when they aren't there. No matter how happy a place seems on the outside, the reality might be very different on the inside. Remember, I thought I was going to Disney

World. PLEASE take care of your family members, especially if they are non-verbal. A few tips I suggest are:

- Make surprise visits.

- Get a lawyer.

- NEVER give up custody or guardianship.

- If you've given it up, get it back. Don't let the institution decide; get legal help.

- Insist on visiting with at least one person who has left the facility.

- If something feels off, check it out.

- Don't just talk, investigate.

* * * * *

Severe depression and anxiety had set in. Between the mind-numbing days, constant threat of shock and mistreatment by abusive staff members, I began to lose hope of ever getting out. I was caught in a circle, waking to the same nightmare every day. Was this really going to be the *rest of my life?*

- Get nervous; tense hands for two seconds...*shock.*

- Get out of bed to use the bathroom...*shock.*

- Miss my mom, crying...*shock.*

I missed my mom desperately, and according to them, miscounting popsicle sticks was a reason to keep me from her. As I looked out the window while counting sticks, I had pangs of desperation.

I wept from the deepest depths of my soul. I knew I was capable of so much more. Several years later, I would become a member of Mensa, for persons with gifted minds. I was intelligent, musically talented, and eager to learn. I wanted *so passionately* to experience real adult life. I was in my thirties. I wanted and needed to experience meaningful work and friendships.

I knew I had love to give, and that I had always been caring. I would make a good friend, if only given the chance. I believe my autism gave me a special way of seeing people and expressing myself that could be a benefit for society; I wasn't the dangerous person they made me out to be. I wanted to have a dog, a cell phone, eat at restaurants, and sleep in on weekends.

Sometimes I would express this to my case manager. You would think my case manager would be impressed that I was articulate and had appropriate goals for life. You would hope she would want me to return to my family and contribute to society rather than be a drain on it.

But I was always met with the same answers: I was not capable of functioning in society safely and that they were saving my life. Although I would outwardly concede, I only accepted her words to appear compliant, and to make the mental pain easier.

I never truly believed this in my heart.

I was continually afraid.

I was terrified of that body-jerking shock that could jolt me at any moment.

I was scared I would grow old and die in that place with no hope and no respect. Would anybody ever know or care? Worse yet, what if I got sick and nobody believed me? Could I be shocked for that?

I saw other sick students suffer. Nobody believed them. They were consequently denied medical care. Most of all, I had that same dreaded belief from when I was a kid: that I would not earn a phone call to my mom one day, and that would cause her to die. That made me sick to my stomach.

While I secretly cried at night, careful to turn my head away from the ever-watching cameras to avoid punishment, I would pray. I would plead with Jesus to please just hold me. To hold me and hug me and comfort me. And one night, He did. I felt a warmth and peace wrap around me. My tears stopped and my body relaxed. I felt all of the weight lift and a joy, peace, and comfort that can't be explained filled my soul. I smiled and held on to it. I knew it was Jesus. There was no other explanation.

* * * * *

I had been in that place for five years, from age 26 to age 30. As the years went by, I worked my way up from short visits and outings with my mom, to day visits at home, and eventually to overnight visits.

These overnight visits were my oasis! For 48 hours I felt like a normal person, able to stand up when I wanted, shower and use the bathroom with privacy, and relax in our quiet condo without being driven to work 16 hours a day on mindless tasks. I could write and sing and relate and show care. When the time would come for me to return, I would cry to my mom, trying to explain to her what my life was like there. She felt powerless but she couldn't bear to hear my pleas because there was nothing she could do. The institution had legal control of me and she could not stop them from taking me back by force if they had to.

Later when I was on one of these overnight home visits, I woke early and for some reason felt compelled to change the television channel from cartoons. As I clicked through the channels, I stopped when I heard someone talking about God and the Bible. I usually avoided televangelists, but this one was simply telling the story of God. I ended up signing up for Bible classes and at the end, I got baptized at the church that I grew up in.

I still felt new to God, since I had strayed for so many years, but I was making my own decision as an adult. I realized He had come to me and had never left my side. What a beautiful security it was to feel heaven if only for a few minutes. He had also come to me as a child several times, as mentioned earlier in this book. To this day, whenever my faith wavers, I think back to those precious moments.

In the last two years of my time in that placement my family worked tirelessly to get guardianship of me so they could end my suffering. Remember all those papers I was made to sign? They had made my mom sign them too. She thought I was practically going to Disney World. She didn't know about all the shocks and abuse at the time she signed the papers. She was only trying to save me from the state hospital.

* * * * *

WARNING: If someone compels you to sign papers that take away your power to help family members, refuse. If you've already signed, get those rights back.

* * * * *

We had signed away all my rights and I had been placed under someone who called himself a guardian. This court-appointed guardian was not a guardian in any way. He was my enemy. But to win would take time. I had already lost so much time. I was too desperate to wait for help. I didn't believe I would ever get out.

One day, my psychologist told me they were going to pull my home visits for the summer because they felt my mom was too lenient with me. Their examples were that she let me drink caffeine and didn't make me go to bed at 10pm. Yup, you read that right. She didn't make her thirty-something-year-old daughter have a bedtime...imagine that. It was considered, in my case manager's words, "running wild" so no more home visits until further notice.

After about two months, I asked if I could go on home visits again.

My psychologist said, "No" and walked away.

I felt a sick feeling in my gut. I started to tremble. I couldn't take it anymore. I was holding on for those visits. They were my reason for not killing myself. I jumped up and started running. I sprinted down the hallways, feeling a rush of freedom as the wind hit my face and the other students watched in awe. I hit the back fire door and flung it open. The alarm went off. I knew I'd better not get caught, or the consequence would be very bad. I hit the big hill of a driveway which led to the highway, and about halfway up, lost all my steam. I continued limping up the hill, but I could hear several pairs of feet coming after me. If I could just reach the highway and get hit by a car, it would all be over.

As I crested the hill, I was knocked off my feet and into the mulch by a large male staff member. The others caught up and held me down. I could only cry noises of despair. I was quickly cuffed into restraints and taken back down the hill. I walked slowly, trying to stall, but they pushed me along. I was brought into another building where the most difficult students were kept, and was restrained on the floor. There I was shocked for all my offenses and then left to sit in my restraints. For the next two months I would have to stay restrained twenty-four hours a day. This also included a helmet, which was a modified red karate helmet with a hockey mask tacked on the front. It had two large locks on the back that tightened around my head. It was the helmet from hell. I couldn't see properly because I couldn't wear my glasses underneath it.

Also, the mask made it hard to breathe. When I exhaled, it felt like my breath was just coming back at me. It was hard not to panic from claustrophobia. They were keeping me like that until my next court date, when they planned to ask the judge to approve me for the higher, more painful level of shocks.

To go to court, my lawyer needed to come see me, and this set off a chain of events that would eventually work in my favor.

When my lawyer came to see me about the new shock proposal, I didn't argue about it. I knew they would win and place me on the stronger devices. However, he also mentioned that my next guardianship hearing was coming and asked me if I wanted to attend. Suddenly a light bulb went off in my head. I needed to get in front of a judge. If I could just tell the judge what was happening, and tell him that I wanted to be my own guardian, maybe he would take pity on me.

Weeks later, I was placed on the new stronger devices. I was scared to get my first shock so I purposely kicked the table so that they would shock me and I could get it over with. This was my new mentality. I was obsessed and worried so much about what I feared, that I wanted to make it happen and be done with it. They shocked me and it hurt, but actually, it wasn't that much worse than the other shocks. It just felt stronger.

I had developed quite a tolerance to pain by this point, out of necessity. I almost laughed, relieved it wasn't that much worse, but I held it in because I knew they would always find a way to hurt me. If I ever seemed unaffected by a consequence, they would search for something else to cause me pain.

My mind was now on my court date. I decided to be optimistic.

My temporary guardianship court date came, and I rode in the minivan, holding my carefully (and secretly) written statement to the judge. I looked out the window and let my eyes unfocus, relaxing my brain. At the court hearing we met up with my lawyer, my mom, and my brother. I was so happy to see them.

During the proceedings there was a lot of back-and-forth with the lawyers until it was my turn to speak. I carefully unfolded my paper and read it clearly to the judge. I explained my desperation, and my wish to be my own guardian. At the end, he asked me if I had written that statement myself. I told him yes. He then turned to the lawyer from my program and remarked on how intelligent I was. Then there was a recess.

During the recess, my lawyer came to me excitedly. He told me that, if I agreed, the judge wanted to appoint my mom or brother as my permanent guardian that day. The judge thought it was ridiculous that this hadn't already been done. My program had been fighting against this for years because they knew if my family became guardians, they would not allow the shock "treatment" to continue.

I was still adamant about becoming my own guardian. I wanted to sign myself out of the program that very day! We went back into the courtroom, and the subject of my family becoming my guardian came up again. I saw my mother start to cry at the thought of continued court dates to decide if I was fit to be my own guardian.

I realized what I needed to do. I wrote a note to my lawyer, telling him I changed my mind. He let the judge know, and in a whirlwind, he was banging his gavel, declaring my mom and my brother as my new *permanent* guardians. That was it. We won! That was the beginning of the end of my captivity in that brutal program.

Immediately, my mom began reviewing my program and making positive changes. They were no longer allowed to put me on that four-point board or to shock me on my hands or feet. She could not take me off the shocks completely yet, because the doctors threatened to kick me out if she did. They told her I would likely accidentally kill myself if she took me home. They made her believe this, but I knew at least things would be better from now on.

I felt a huge sense of relief knowing that my mom could now protect me from at least some of the worst of it. My depression and anxiety lessened but my patience to leave that place was still short.

After court, my family began talking to my state workers about getting me into a new program. We finally had a meeting set up with the new placement and all I had to do was wait. Around the same time, I had to have surgery. Months earlier, I had fractured my thumb while playing in the gym. The program nurses did not take my complaints of pain seriously and they started to insinuate that if I kept complaining, I would be charged with making "medical complaints without foundation." So I stopped mentioning it. Later, on a home visit, my mom took me to the doctor where a simple x-ray revealed my broken thumb. I was placed in a cast but the damage had been done. I needed surgery to correct it. I hoped this would not slow down my discharge.

Meeting day with my new program director came in February 2009. The man *seemed* nice. He whispered to me that he was going to get me out. My new placement was all the way in Florida; I preferred going home, but at that point I didn't care. I wanted out! The cold spring days seemed to go by so slowly until my scheduled discharge date of April 1, 2009. April Fool's Day came, and no joke, I was discharged.

My case manager flew with me and the recruiter to Tampa airport. When we got outside in Florida, the weather was sunny and beautiful. The landscape looked rich and green and there were palm trees! This was a stark contrast from the long, wet, cold spring we were having up north. I smiled at the sunshine, feeling light as a feather. We got in the rented car and drove for over an hour. The recruiter played terrible disco music for the entire ride, but I didn't even care. I was *free*.

CHAPTER 22

Freedom Was Not Instant

"Bit by bit, as I was treated with dignity, I
began to live and relate and love."

We finally pulled into the front gate of my new program location and the recruiter pointed out the cows and horses that were kept towards the front of the property. All I could see for miles was open land dotted with trees covered in Spanish moss. As we began our drive down the three-mile driveway, I thought to myself that if things went wrong here, it would be very hard to run away. Every direction looked the same!

Once we pulled onto the sprawling campus, I was taken to the nurses station for the usual check-in process, including the dreaded body search. I noticed right away that the nurse *asked* me to do things instead of directing me.

Already I was being treated with a level of dignity that I had been denied for the past seven years.

Acclimating to my new placement was very difficult. I was returning to an old life that I had only dreamed of experiencing again. For seven years I had existed in a frozen state, barely surviving, while the world went on without me. Up until my last days at the previous facility, I had been on the shock program—even with my mother's intervention. I was very used to wearing the devices which served as a constant reminder for me to toe the line.

To be free of them all of a sudden felt, well, scary. The shock program was the only form of redirection I knew. I had been immersed in the culture and though unspeakably cruel, it had become familiar, a way of life for me.

I had preserved that small part of me that remained unchanged, carefully wrapped and protected for a later time. Now that I was here, I took my time to see if it was safe to slowly unfold that protective layer that surrounded my true spirit. This would all mean taking a series of risks.

I had been told for years that I could not handle being off the shocks, and that I would likely hurt myself, or even take my own life accidently. This nonsense arose because they only saw me for my misunderstood behaviors. I had been brainwashed not to trust myself, but to rely solely on others who controlled me externally. I was never allowed to express my feelings or taught coping skills. I was only dealt with using consequences and punishments, creating a vicious cycle, repeating the same pattern of behaviors instead of progressing and moving forward toward a goal of independence at the age of 33. I was simply not prepared for life outside of that environment.

Now I could do absolutely anything: yell, tense my hands, get out of my seat without permission, tell the staff "no." I was listened to, respected, and treated as a person.

And although there were rules I had to follow—wise and sensible ones this time—there would be no ensuing electric shock as a result of breaking them. At the same time, unbeknownst to me, I was learning positive reinforcement as a healthy way of managing my behaviors.

It was all too much. I was so conditioned that I couldn't handle the freedom.

My brother had visited before I came to this facility. He thoroughly investigated rather than just taking the surface tour. He told me it was a beautiful place. It didn't disappoint.

Set deep in the Florida countryside, I would joke that there was nothing but cows and oranges around us. I first noticed the lack of busy and overwhelming decor everywhere. It was freeing. No Coca-Cola staircase here. No Mickey Mouse rooms. We lived in cabins painted in natural muted colors. This was a drastic change and relief to my senses.

I had gotten used to the over-stimulating and fake environment at my last place and even though it was detrimental, it was what I knew. Walls painted in bright pinks and purples, giant cartoon-like statues around every corner with each room having a theme. My bedroom had been all pink with itchy lacy throw pillows that had to be placed on the bed. The walls had a wide purple stripe encircling the room. There were decorative dolls on the shelves and sequined lamps. Blech...all I wanted was a cool, calm place to call my own and relax my brain.

And I found it here.

I loved the fact that we had to walk outside between buildings to go to work and lunch. The old program made going outside a reward that I had to earn.

Being outdoors was very important to me and my mental health. I needed it. All of this sudden freedom, where I could walk outside and sit on the porch without having to earn it felt *incredibly* liberating, while at the same time feeling out of place. Cruel and inappropriate treatment had me used to being kept inside. My previous captors had convinced me the simple act of going out the door was wrong.

Birds and squirrels and deer played. So could I.

The sun was bright and high in the sky. It warmed me.

This was my new life I had been praying for.

Why wasn't I content? Could I believe it? Would this work? Could I live with such freedom or did I need the shocks? I actually had been brainwashed. I was used to being told what to do every step of the way, from getting permission to get out of bed in the morning until I was directed to get into bed at night. The whole day I was told where to stand, how to walk, when I could eat, drink, use the bathroom and for how long. I was told when I could speak, take a break, exactly what and how much/little I could eat. Every aspect of my life was dictated by a horribly impersonal program and its staff.

Now, with all of the sudden freedom, I felt manic—like when you give a small child an entire bag of Halloween candy and they are so excited they don't know what to do with themselves. That was me. Freedom was the candy.

But I was ready to learn and live that freedom.

These opposite and conflicting emotions of being happy yet afraid caused me quite understandable stress. I had so much unlearning to do. I had been programmed, and I was just now realizing this. I was wound tight and always trying to keep and look busy while the clients and staff around me looked so relaxed. They would sit for hours on the weekend and watch movies on the couch. I couldn't understand this. I needed to be busy because at the last facility we were never allowed to sit idle for more than a few minutes. The monitoring department who watched the cameras would call and warn the staff that we were not allowed leisure time. Breaks had to be earned in 10-minute increments.

There was no such thing as a relaxing weekend or evening on the couch. "Get them up!" they would demand. "Make them work on a task!" We were constantly dusting things that had just been dusted, or vacuuming a clean floor just to have work to do.

When I would try to relax I would swear I'd hear the phone ringing in my mind, knowing I was about to be yelled at to get up and clean something. At first I dealt with this anxiety by always keeping myself busy so that I wouldn't be yelled at and directed. This was wrong and my spirit knew it. Every time I heard the sound of a velcro wallet opening I would stiffen up and prepare myself for a shock because they had used velcro to keep our remote boxes closed when we were not in trouble. To this day, the sound of velcro makes me jump.

I no longer knew how to just sit and be with myself. But I would LEARN! I never had been given the chance to sit and think about goals, likes, dislikes, my future, or who I was. I had been institutionalized since I was a teen. Now I was an adult and I was not sure of my identity. I never had that chance to progress through adulthood.

With all of that discomfort, I pushed through, believing that I could re-enter the life I once knew. Staffers helped me. Imagine that! They helped me!

Although I felt isolated from the other clients, having gone through such a rare traumatic experience, I tried my best to answer them when they spoke to me. I was determined to get along with them.

I had to intently focus and keep reminding myself that I was not "there" anymore. I had to push forward and not get caught up in my past because the painful memories could easily engulf me. Their program had worked...I was convinced their rules were right. But my spirit knew better. And step-by-step I would find my way.

I even emailed my old case manager from time to time and would tell her if I had gotten in trouble. I had such extreme feelings of guilt I believed I needed to confess them to her. What if they were right? What if I could not survive under my own control?

CHAPTER 23

Feeling More Like the Adult I Was Supposed to Be

"I was officially diagnosed with autism [and] music made its way back into my life."

Soon I was getting frustrated with noise made by the other clients and even the staff. We would be gathered in the living room and clients would play music on the big speaker. They would joke with each other, being loud and rambunctious. The staff would yell to each other across the room.

This would lead me to want to get away from the area, and my staff often wouldn't let me leave. I would run off and try to find a place to hide. They didn't understand or care how badly I suffered.

It usually felt like my discomfort was nothing more than an inconvenience to the staff. I felt alone and afraid because they were in charge and I was completely dependent on them. If they didn't care, who would? I would try to escape the madness and when they would stop me I ended up biting myself or banging my head. It was just a natural reaction. I felt like a jumpy, anxious squirrel who had been trapped.

Despite all that, I had an assigned 1:1 staff member who really took the time to understand and care for me. But there were other staff working in the program who felt like they needed to show me who was boss, to establish their dominance. They would preemptively grab me and threaten me under their breath, or take away something that belonged to me, like the snacks my case manager had given me for the weekend. These holdovers from the previous cruelty caused me to melt down.

I was now getting restrained a lot.

Back to the blue mats.

Was I headed back to the torture?

Unscrupulous staff would do things like bend my fingers back or pinch me to try and control me. Only I was immune to such tactics by now, having been shocked with electrodes for the last seven years. My pain tolerance was high. I could handle the physical pain, but it still took an emotional toll on me, that they would do this thinking they were succeeding in hurting me.

I was tired of abuse. I was tired of being the victim. I would report these things to the abuse hotline, but nothing was ever done to the staff that hurt me. I wasn't surprised. That had been my experience.

I was being seen by different doctors who officially diagnosed me with autism. When I found out, I didn't want to believe I had autism and I really didn't acknowledge the fact at first. I felt embarrassed. I felt like people would look at me weirdly if they knew that about me. Doubt and anger settled in and it took me a while to process my diagnosis. My old program did not believe in diagnoses. I had gotten too used to the idea that I was just a badly behaved person.

My mom sent me articles to read so I could "learn more about myself," she would say. As I read them, I realized...this *was* me. Even the parts about me trying to cover it up and blend in was common among girls with autism. What I read was also my story. I started to feel relieved and more accepting of myself.

As I understood more, I had fewer problems with acting out. I began to recognize when I was getting overwhelmed and, with the help of my staff, was able to remove myself from situations. FINALLY, I HAD HELP!

I started talking more about how I was feeling to the people I trusted.

I learned to ask questions if I didn't understand what someone's facial expression meant.

Instead of melting down all the time, I learned actions that would help me master my emotions and my interactions with others.

I was also put back on some medications—appropriate ones this time, rather than the ridiculously high dosages I was on at the state hospital. The medicine helped me control my tics and obsessions.

I enjoyed plentiful energy and played basketball and volleyball. I would go for long walks and bike rides. My doctor also thought it would be helpful if I got my own emotional support dog. That had been my dream for years! I worked really hard to show I would be a good caretaker. Finally, the day came. A woman from the local poodle rescue came with a little black dog named Boomer. He was an old dog who had recently lost his owner. He was gentle and sweet. We bonded quickly and soon he was following me around the cabin where I lived. My little black shadow.

A year after I arrived at my new place, I began to have nightmares about the shocks at my last placement. Every night I would dream about getting shocked, or trying to get to a phone to call my mom, or trying to run away. The nightmares were torturously vivid and I would wake up tormented. These dreams became a regular part of my life. Even though I was away from those people, they were still hurting me.

I felt angry about what I went through and I started to speak publicly about what had happened to me. At first I kept it anonymous, but staff from my old placement quickly guessed it was me and I decided I wouldn't hide. I wanted the world to know that I was a real person telling the truth about what went on behind those brightly painted Mickey Mouse walls.

I also started playing music again. My mom shipped my old keyboard to me and I picked right up where I had left off from that night at the high school talent show. The music was right there waiting for me, eager to pour out. Songs I had been listening to for years were waiting at my fingertips.

The first song I played was Sarah McLachlan's "Angel," a song which had comforted me during those horrid times.

Soon after getting my keyboard, I picked up my iPad, propped it up with some books, and recorded videos of me playing. Then I uploaded them to YouTube. A few days later I looked at my channel and saw that people were starting to watch my videos from all around the world. This was so exciting!

I was actually reaching the world from my little place among the cows and oranges. I posted more videos and watched the world come to *me*. I had been separated for so long from everyone—family, friends, society. It pained me for years to know I had something inside to share, but that I wasn't allowed to. I was locked away both physically and mentally. Now, I was making a small step out of the dark.

Music was therapeutic for me and for my listeners. It brought me back to my childhood, comforted my body, and made me feel calm. It focused me when I felt scattered, and I was able to just be still when the music from my piano entered my ears.

CHAPTER 24

Freedom Must Be Learned, Too

"Don't you ever apologize for taking up space in this world.
You have a place here just like anyone else."

Bit by bit, action by action, my days got better. I gained more control over my impulses.

I was learning to enjoy the freedom that came with that, and with every other feature of being able to make a lot of my own decisions. Going out to the store and shopping for myself became a favorite activity. I worked at my vocational job—which in the beginning was simply shredding paperwork, but at least I was getting paid minimum wage and not pennies. I was allowed to hold my own money and I learned to budget for things I wanted. I felt empowered.

As a 33-year-old woman, I was coming into my own. My confidence grew with each wise choice. I was becoming more like the adult I was supposed to be.

Nights, however, were a different story. My dreams continued to be dominated by the shocks. I would wake feeling like I had fought in a wrestling match all night long, tense and sore from clenching my muscles. I wanted it to end. I figured I was stuck this way for life.

I wanted the abusers to acknowledge what they had done to me. I started to see a counselor about it, but I have never liked counseling, and this counselor wasn't very helpful. Eventually she moved away and I never saw anyone else.

I realized I function much better when I approach an issue in the moment. I have a hard time expressing what I am going through unless it is happening right then. I find I express myself much better through writing, music, or art rather than talking to someone.

Music was slowly making its way back into my life. I decided I wanted to learn the guitar, so I bought a ukulele. Why a ukulele? Because I figured with its smaller size and only four strings, it would help get my hands used to the motions of playing guitar without being too overwhelming. It turned out to be a sound idea. Once I had a grasp of the ukulele, I bought a small guitar. I started teaching myself chords by watching YouTube videos and using a guitar app on my phone.

Then one day my case manager called me up to the dining room and said she needed to talk to me. When I entered, several people I did not recognize were sitting there. One of the other case managers had arranged for me to receive the instrument of a retired symphony violinist. She was there to pass it down to me, as she could no longer play. Everyone was crying; it was very emotional. I was crying with happiness. The fact that all these people saw in me something deserving of such a gift was beyond words. They were seeing and showing what I knew was inside of me.

I held the violin in my hands and took in its beauty. It was made of dark wood, and was worn around the fingerboard from years of being played. I was told the violin was very old and special. They asked me to play something. I was on the spot...it had been years since I had seen a violin. I slowly placed it under my chin and rested it on my shoulder. A familiar warmth washed over me. I remembered that feeling from when I was a kid, playing in that sunny corner at school.

I raised the bow, trying to recall a line of music. I ran the bow across the lowest string. A deep resonating tone came out. I felt the vibrations in my shoulder and face. My body relaxed and I started to play my own song, making it up as I went. This violin had an exemplary tone, deep and sweet. It felt like it personally fit my hands, like it had been worn to my own specifications. I did not know how to thank that woman enough. I worry to this day that she does not know how much I appreciate her gift.

* * * * *

As time passed I kept speaking out online about my treatment at my previous placement. I started to make friends who supported me in my effort to stop the cruelty from happening to others. I was invited to speak a few times at conventions and panels about institutional abuse. I was honored to have those opportunities, and even more glad that the truth was spreading. Maybe freedom could come for more victims.

I was meeting many people and my confidence grew with each encounter. My social skills were also improving since I was finally able to have real world practice interacting with people. Starting and maintaining conversations, even the boring ones, got easier. I learned how to navigate my way through chit-chat and small talk to get to the topics I was actually interested in. I was also going on home visits four times a year. I would fly home with a staff member and my emotional support dog Boomer and stay with my mom for a week or so. I loved those visits. Unlike my last place, I did not dread coming back to Florida. It was becoming more and more my home—I had a safe place with my mother and in my own home.

Boomer was old, and one day while I was at home on a visit, he got very sick. He was struggling to breathe. We rushed him to the vet, but he was in heart failure and there wasn't anything they could do. That day, I had to make the very tough decision to let him go. I stayed with him the whole time, wanting him to know he was loved until the very end. I was heartsick afterward. I couldn't eat. I started obsessing over the fact that maybe he would have recovered and I shouldn't have let him go. No amount of reassurance helped. I cried for days. Arriving back in Florida was hard, seeing his bowls and toys laid out on the floor.

After a couple months, I started to feel well enough to open my heart to another dog. When I saw little Yerby's face on the rescue website, I knew he was mine. The woman who was caring for him was apprehensive at first. He was known as a bit of a troublemaker who just needed to be understood. Did I ever understand that! I told the woman that I was a bit of a complexity myself, and that I believed we would get along perfectly. She laughed and agreed. After bringing Yerby home, the smile returned to my face. He was curly and warm and smelled like honey. I loved to rub my face in his curly fur. He definitely was a troublemaker, and he gave me many laughs as well as kept me on my toes. But he also knew when I needed comforting, and he was always there for me at those times.

* * * * *

One evening, soon after Yerby came home, I was watching *Jeopardy!* with my staff member. I was getting so many questions...er...answers right. She was impressed and remarked, "You need to try out for this show!" Being someone who was starting to try new things, I searched the internet on how to become a *Jeopardy!* contestant. This led me down a rabbit hole of IQ testing sites and logic quizzes.

Then I saw it: the practice test for admission to American Mensa, a prestigious high IQ society. I remember kids trying to get into Mensa when I was in high school, and my mom used to tell me I should try for it.

There was no way...was there?

I paid the fee and took the practice test. My results said that I had a highly likely chance of passing the real test. I was wary that they might tell everybody that, but I still wanted to try the real thing. Many people would assume I had little chance to qualify. I wanted to prove to them I could.

The doubters even tried to prepare me for my coming failure. This motivated me even more to do well. The day of the test came and on the way to the library, I drank a strong coffee and ate a handful of nuts for lasting energy. The room was warm with one big table around which four of us candidates sat. The woman giving the test was very strict but kind.

The test was hard. Not because you needed to have a lot of education, but because you needed to know how to solve problems quickly. You needed to be logical and have a good memory. And again, you needed to work very quickly. There was barely enough time to finish each section, so you needed to be sure of yourself. After the test, I was sweating but I felt good. I knew I had done the best of my ability.

A long two weeks later, I received an email: "Congratulations...!"

I was over the moon!! I was so happy that all those people who called me stupid were wrong. In order to make it into Mensa your IQ needs to be in the top two percent of people in the world. It was a crowning achievement.

* * * * *

I had also set up a Facebook account and was adding new friends every day. Most of them I met through my advocacy against skin shock and institutional abuse.

One day, I had a difference of opinion with one of these "friends." This person immediately bombarded me with nasty posts and messages. I couldn't block them fast enough. I started crying hysterically. It felt like I was facing the school bullies all over again. They wouldn't stop. I had to block all of these people. They still tried other ways to get through to me. I was sick to my stomach.

I was just starting to trust people and to think I understood. And then I had been betrayed. I decided I would never have another friend.

My illogical thinking became a blessing in disguise. Trust was not an all-or-nothing thing; friends were not all-or-nothing relationships. I had to discern who to trust, who to try to befriend, and who to go deeper with. I started to learn to lean on my insights and remember that my worth was in God.

I grew a new set of social skills: to stop letting others have all the influence on my values. I started forming opinions of my own. As I did that, my confidence and wisdom grew. The staff members even picked up on it and started to treat me differently. I was able to stand up to them and insist on being treated fairly. I was finding my voice!

CHAPTER 25

Music Gave Me My Voice

*"God gave me the gift of music; I used it to share His
light, posting a new song almost every day."*

My piano videos were doing well on YouTube. I could listen to a song, and in
my mind the right notes would appear. God had given me the gift of music
and I wanted to use it to share His light.

I was learning a new song almost every day and posting it. I had started
taking lessons at a music school about an hour away. I loved my teacher.
She was more like a mentor, and she guided me through whatever musical
project I was up to.

She helped me stretch and grow as a musician. As I was becoming more
and more expressive, I started to want to write my own songs. My teacher was
so excited that I wanted to take this step. She equipped me for it. We started
brainstorming ideas of things to write about. One night soon after, I couldn't
fall asleep, and then poetic words started coming into my mind. I grabbed
my guitar and started working out the words into rhythms and chords. In no
time, I had written a complete song.

I was so excited, I called my mom, waking her up. I sang her my song.
She couldn't really hear it well over the phone, but she heard my excitement
and encouraged me anyway. The following week I played it for my teacher.
Tears welled up in her eyes. My song was called "When You Were Born." It
was about bullies and trials in life, but in the end you are only getting older
so you need to let those hard memories go in favor of laughter, love, and life.
The song summed up the realizations I had been having, that I was getting
older and it was time I live my life fully without my past holding me back. I
believed others would identify with the song too.

That year my music school held a "Got Talent" competition. I auditioned, singing my original song. After my audition, I was preparing to leave when one of the judges ran up to me. I could tell she was fancy, just by the way she dressed and carried herself. I liked her instantly, not because of her fanciness, but because of her spirit. She introduced herself, and began to tell me how much she loved my song. She wanted to give me her card because she wanted to have me on her local radio show.

Wow! I tried to be cool in the moment, but on the inside I was jumping up and down. I thanked her and promised I'd stay in contact. I didn't win the competition, but something much bigger came out of it. I made a connection and gained opportunities I never would have had if I hadn't put myself out there and taken a chance. If I had gotten upset and worried that I might not win the competition, I would have missed out. I got to be on the radio and sing my song; I was even invited to be on the local version of *The View*. Again I got to sing my song and tell my story. I was starting to envision a future for myself.

I started a second YouTube channel called *Jen Adventures TV* where I made little skits and did product reviews. It was so much fun. I felt like I could let my creativity out and grow. It was like writing my childhood family newspaper, the *Msumba Magnificent*, all over again. It was fun but just a hobby at that point.

I did not know where it would lead to, if anywhere. Little did I know I was in for an awesome ride.

* * * * *

One day, my dog Yerby and I were in the office of one of the administrative staff. Next door, the newly hired staff were going through training. Suddenly, Yerby took off and ran into that other room. He ran right to one of the female staff and sat by her feet. She was delighted, saying that he looked just like her dog Brody. She seemed like such a kind soul. I told her, "I hope you get to be my staff." She smiled a bright smile and said "I hope so too." Two weeks later on a Saturday, Lindsay walked into my life.

On Sundays we had the option to attend one of the local churches. Even though I had become a Christian, I had a fear of church. It gave me anxiety because I had been worrying about devils since I was little.

՝ Every week, my staffer Lindsay would ask me if I wanted to go to church and I would say, "Maybe next time." Weeks passed, and I gave into a growing urge to give church a try.

When we arrived, everyone was so kind. They treated me like they already knew me! I got my coffee and donut and took a seat. Worship began. I was blown away. It was amazing! The music was beautiful. Praising God together with other believers felt like nothing I had ever experienced. I watched the band carefully, wishing I could be a part of it.

After worship we sat for announcements. Wouldn't you know it: they were holding auditions for the worship team! I could barely stay in my seat. I was so excited. After the message I told Lindsay, "I *have* to do this." She introduced me to the worship leader and told him I played the piano or "keys" as they called it.

He said, "We have been looking for a keys player!"

Long story short, I passed my audition and became a member of the worship team. I was part of a team!

Right away they accepted me as family. We had lots of get-togethers and time rehearsing together. Sometimes I would start to cry, I was so happy and full. These friends were different. They weren't just my friends because they felt bad for me or I had something they wanted, they were *true*.

If I made a mistake, they would forgive me and move on. They took the time to get to know and understand me and my autism. We grew give-and-take relationships and reciprocal appreciation for each other.

I have learned that we *all* have quirky things about us. Our worship leader is scared of frogs. Our guitar player is blind in one eye. We all had things about us that were hard, but together we were strong. I started to feel very safe. I had a routine that included learning songs all week, rehearsal on Thursdays, and arriving for soundcheck early on Sundays. I feel like a real honest adult in the world. What a gift. My days were happy and full. My

YouTube channel was gaining more and more followers. With the help of my brother I decided to rename it *Rebranding Autism,* because I was showing it's okay to get out in the world and try new things. People with autism are capable of so much more than the stereotypes. Later I would change the name of my channel to simply *Jennifer Msumba.*

Instead of copying my favorite YouTubers, I decided to just be myself. If people liked it, great; and if they didn't, that was okay too. I had learned that not everyone is going to like you in this world, and that's okay. At the time of this writing I have almost 32,000 followers.

On my newly named channel I started talking more openly about my autism and my life experiences. I thought these videos may not do well, but people were commenting on how much it had helped them. This motivated me to make more videos where I could help people going through things similar to what I was going through. I wanted to be a positive light. I prayed to God to help me show His love and to be true and have humility. To this day, that is my prayer.

From my channel, a major television network discovered me and asked me to be on *The Employables,* a show that documented people with autism and/or Tourette's syndrome searching for employment. That was something I wanted as well, a job out in the community. I really wanted to get a job serving coffee. I love coffee and I thought I would make a great barista and serve with a smile. But I ended up getting turned down.

I was able to find a volunteer job at a nearby animal shelter, where I walked and bathed dogs and cleaned the cat rooms. It was hard work but the animals made it all worth it. Filming for *The Employables* was so much fun. Lindsay agreed to film with me as my staffer. We got treated like stars. There were camera operators and a producer and we had a personal assistant who would go out and get us whatever we wanted for lunch and coffee and snacks.

The crew was really kind and well trained. They were also sensitive to my needs and very considerate. We all had fun together and I am still friends with some of them to this day. I learned a lot about the art of production: filming, lighting, and audio.

All these skills would prove useful for me with my YouTube channel and filmmaking aspirations. After we wrapped filming, I had the idea that I wanted to start making short films. I wanted to write stories and see them come to life. I started learning everything I could about filmmaking and storytelling. I began to keep a notebook where I wrote down story ideas.

One idea stood out to me. It was going to be a story about kids in a psychiatric unit, who were really bored from the mundane days. Each would be in his or her own world dealing with their own struggles. Then one boy would get an idea that would change everything. I titled it *The Dayroom*.

* * * * *

Around that time, Yerby was starting to lose weight and did not want to eat. This went on for months, until he started having seizures that even medicine couldn't stop. I knew in my heart what was happening, but I didn't want to believe it. He spent several nights at the vet and then came home. After church one day I came home and he couldn't stand up. He was turning in circles and confused. I started crying from the bottom of my soul. I knew it was his time. The doctors had tried everything. Last time that situation happened, I had my mom with me for comfort and support. But I was all the way in Florida without her. Then I remembered. I had my church family. I called my friend Amanda and she came right over. She drove with me solemnly to the animal hospital where they evaluated Yerby. They sadly agreed it was his time. I cried so hard I hurt for days after. But Amanda and all my friends and staff were there.

Right before that happened, I had attended a huge conference in Orlando, Florida called Playlist Live. It's a place for online creators to meet and learn and collaborate. I got to meet other YouTubers who talked about autism. I thought they were fun and wanted to hang out with them, but didn't know how to ask. I had learned over time that it's not good to just force your way into people's business. So I sat in one of the learning panels, trying to think up a strategy. My whole life had been a game of strategy, always trying to figure out how I was going to navigate my way around a confusing and overwhelming world. Then I had an idea. I would write them a note, old school style, asking if they wanted to hang out. Then I put a "circle yes or no" option at the bottom. Genius. I passed it to one of them. They read it and laughed out loud. Not at me, but with me.

"Duh!" they wrote back, "Of course!"

We spent the weekend getting to know each other, and I was sad when it was time to say goodbye. But they lived only about three hours away and I knew I would see them again.

Time passed after losing Yerby, and I was feeling lonely for a canine friend. I decided it was time to open my heart to another sweet pup. I searched for days online, filling out applications for different dogs. I kept getting denied. As I refreshed the rescue site again and again, a new face popped up. It was a chubby sweet Cockapoo girl named Angel. That time, I sent an email to the rescue in addition to filling out the application. Thirty minutes later, a kind woman called me. She had read my email and was intrigued. She had lots of questions about my living situation and ability to care for Angel. She explained to me that Angel needed to be on a careful diet to lose weight and she wanted to know if I was ready to take care of her.

I was SO ready. She decided to give me a chance. She said she felt God had brought us together. Either way, I was beginning to see how God was bringing my life together. He brought me to this place, and even though it was so far from my family, He provided me with another family to watch over me. He had never left me; even when I was in the depths of despair, He held me. Now my blessings were overflowing.

A few days later I brought Angel home, but we thought she looked more like a Lemonade. Besides, what other dog do you know that was named Lemonade? But I can't really take the credit for the name; one of my staff, Lori, and I had heard it once on a television show where there was a mini horse named Lemonade. We thought that was the cutest.

Lemonade had been through a lot. She was living with an older couple and the wife passed away. After that, she went through a time of neglect. She had a hard time trusting me at first. We took our time with each other and I would whisper in her ear that I promised to take care of her. Sweet girl. She has been my comfort and companion animal ever since. Now I had wonderful human companions and a canine companion.

My YouTube channel was starting to really take off. I started to get nervous, knowing that as a channel grows, so do the people that don't like you. I braced myself for cruel comments. I am so sensitive, I didn't know how I would handle it, but I would be strong. Surprisingly the mean comments have been few and far between so far. I hope it stays that way, but you never know. I keep the channel going because of the people who watch. They write to me and tell me how much I have helped them and given them hope. I realized that my channel was no longer just something I did for fun, but that I was affecting real people. I realize I have a great responsibility. All that I have been through has prepared me, though.

My mom and brother have also been a huge part of me becoming responsible. They encourage me to make phone calls to the bank and other companies on my own. They teach me to be responsible with my money but are always there to step in when I need it. My brother taught me to be bold and ask for things I want. "It's free to ask," he always says. "The worst that can happen is they say no"

We are very close. We enjoy reminiscing and laughing about the old days.

* * * * *

When COVID-19 hit, I did not know what I was going to do. Since I live in what's considered a long-term care facility, I haven't been allowed to leave. Not even my brother can fix that for me. I can't see my church friends or fly home to hug my mom. After a time of feeling bad for myself, I pulled it together and let the free time become a good thing. I started writing great quantities of music, and now this book. It has been a hard time for everyone. But this is a test...and I'm gonna pass. I am not just going to pass, but I am going to thrive. I'm done with merely surviving. I have so much to share. There is so much God has placed inside of me. I pray to Him every day that He helps me to shine His light for all to see and do the job that He gave me.

One day, years ago, my mom and I were in the grocery store. It was very busy and crowded, and I kept apologizing for getting in people's way. Every time they wanted to get where I was standing, I jumped out of their way and said sorry. Finally, my mom got so tired of this, she pulled me aside. She said to me in a firm voice as she gripped my arm, "Don't you ever apologize for taking up space in this world. You have a place here just like anyone else. You are just as important as anyone else." Her words hit me profoundly. She had tried to instill this in me for so many years, but with the physical example, it finally clicked. I never have forgotten her words. Promise me you won't forget them either.

CHAPTER 26

Some Advice–Others Have Walked Before You

"Look at their eyebrows."

Where do I want to go from here?

I want to live life beyond a facility. I want to own my own house and hire whoever I want to be my staff. I want to go fishing *a lot*, write music, maybe even become a speaker and live a quiet life in between. Most of all, I want to live for God and the plan He has for me. I will not be afraid. Here are seven specific goals I have for myself, and highly recommend for others:

1. Have a Positive Mindset

As a teenager, when I thought of my future, I drew a huge blank. I didn't see college, work, and family. I instinctively knew I wasn't typical. I wish I had known it was okay to have an alternative future. That I didn't have to get married or have romantic relationships, and that I had talents worth developing, like my music and creativity.

I didn't really try to develop these, but I can do that now. I wasted all those years living up to the wrong expectations. I took to heart all the times people told me I didn't matter or wasn't intelligent. They were wrong!

If you are a teenager or young adult, please know that you deserve to choose a fulfilling life as much as anyone else. Even if you are different from most people your age, you can create a beautiful life for yourself. Surround yourself with positive friends and family. Refuse to dwell on negative things, because there are more good things in this world than bad.

Guard your heart and be mindful of what you let into your eyes and ears, whether that be music or books or what you watch on TV. What you allow in affects your heart. For example, when I stopped listening to music that cursed and talked about bad things, my mind started to feel better, I was less anxious and I became more positive.

2. Grow Your Social Skills

I learned my social skills through trial, and *much* error. I don't want you to go through as much error as I did. Keep this in mind: the majority of the time, people are thinking of themselves, not you. You are actually not as important to most people as you think you are. But in the best way!

People are usually not thinking about what you look like or that odd thing you just said. They are thinking about their own lives, like what's for dinner or when is their next job promotion. If you think someone is giving you a mean face, they are probably just thinking about how they have to go home to clean out the garage. Remind yourself of this next time you feel self-conscious in a crowd.

Also, if you find someone you really want to be friends with, try hard not to overwhelm them with your enthusiasm. Even though you have the best intentions, it can overwhelm them and maybe even seem creepy. I used to push many potential friends away because of this. Those of us with autism may get really excited and focused on a topic or task. And if that includes another human, you have to learn to tone it down.

Why? Relationships take time for *everybody*. When you suspect you are becoming too much for someone, you might be. I like to navigate this by asking a trusted friend or family member if they think I am being "too much." For example, I will ask them how long I should wait between text messages, or if it's okay to approach someone if they seem busy. Don't be afraid to ask for help with this. It can save you a lot of heartache.

3. Use Eye Contact

This can be a tricky subject. Eye contact is hard. It hurts. It feels like car headlights are flooding your brain and you can no longer think. Most people with autism believe that you shouldn't ever feel forced to make eye contact. And in general, I feel this is true. However, if you never attempt to make eye contact, you might miss out. I do not like eye contact, and for a long time I avoided it with most people. But I started to realize that I was not able to connect with the people I really wanted to connect with. Many people take my lack of eye contact as lack of interest in them. If they spoke to me and I looked at the ground, it communicated to them that I didn't care or wasn't listening. I knew that wasn't true, but they didn't.

I started an experiment and began making myself make some eye contact when talking to people. I used the trick of not really looking into their eyes but looking at their eyebrows. Haha, I beat the system! In their mind, I was making eye contact. My friendships grew. People wanted to have conversations with me, and they built up trust with me. Eye contact is part of life; you don't have to partake, but you just may be missing out on making a great connection.

4. Make Friends

When you are very young, making friends is more straightforward. If you both like cars—bam, you run off and play cars together. I know it is still hard for some kids, but the rules are more clear. As you get older, the rules become more subtle. Kids break off into groups and cliques based on perceptions, such as how cool or popular they are. Most of the time that system is wrong! So find caring people—people you can show interest in who show interest in you. Otherwise you settle for a ridiculous system to navigate.

I really did not understand cliques when I was in school and I also was not maturing as fast as the other kids. I didn't want to talk about boys or hang out at football games or go to parties. I wanted to play Barbies or Nintendo at home. I managed to have friends at school, but outside of school I was alone. When I got to be an adult, I really had the desire to make friends of my own.

Not just staff members who, even though they truly liked me, were being paid to spend time with me.

I grew my first "outside" friends by joining my church worship team. Even though I have autism and a different life than they do, we have something in common and that is our love for music and the Lord. It makes it much easier to make friends if you have something in common.

If you are interested in making friends, I would suggest getting into some group or club or job where you all have a common interest. This gives you something to talk about and it is not so stressful trying to come up with conversational topics. The conversations happen more organically, and soon you are comfortable around each other and can talk about a range of things, helping you grow close. Maybe you could also use that eye contact trick!

5. Work with Your Family, Friends, and Caregivers

I can't speak for everyone with autism, but I know things for me are not always as they seem. What I mean is a lot of times I will get very upset and have a meltdown but it has nothing to do with the current situation. A lot of times I will fixate on something that happened from the day before, or something I hear that is so quiet no one else hears it. I will hold it in as long as I can, and when it finally comes out it might seem completely out of nowhere.

So ask your family and friends to help you figure out what's wrong and track back to what happened in the past to set it off. Or look around for something that is barely perceivable to you.

I urge family members and friends to keep an open mind when your loved one gets upset and not assume they are trying to get out of something, or act out just to act out. There is usually a tangible reason.

Also, if your loved one is having a meltdown or hard time, find a way to help. I know for me it makes it worse when people keep repeating at me to calm down or keep touching me, even in a kind way. When I'm like that I just need them to be close, but still give me space to calm down. That is what has always been most helpful. It helps me calm down if I can do something repeatedly, like squeeze a Jabberball or organize a deck of cards by number and suit.

Also, if I'm feeling destructive, then it helps if I have magazines to rip or a cardboard box out of the trash. Something I can completely destroy to get my energy out. These are just some examples I wanted to share.

6. Refuse Self-Harm

Hurting myself is something I've struggled with my entire life, and it's no wonder due to the people in the institutions where I spent so much time. They made me feel useless! I have always had impulses to hit my head or bite myself. Sometimes I get this urge when I am very excited and happy, and sometimes when I am very frustrated and upset. It seems to be when I am feeling an extreme emotion and I don't know where to put it all. There is so much wanting to burst out that I can't contain it. Something about banging my head is actually soothing. It calms me because I have another strong feeling to counteract the one I am trying to manage. This in turn creates a balance for me and I feel more even-keeled.

I know this is harmful, but in those moments it is an impulse I don't know how to stop. It helps me if I have an alternative to hurting myself that still feels strong. Like biting into something very chewy, hitting my head into a pillow, jumping up and down, or clapping loudly. Something that my body really can feel. These are things I try to do instead, and the more I practice them, the more I am able to do them instead of harming myself.

7. Follow Your Dreams

My goal in writing this book is to show the world the power of people with autism. I hope to help bridge the gap between people with autism and their friends, teachers, and family. Autistic people should not be underestimated. The days of abusive treatments need to end and we should have the opportunity to be integrated into society.

God made each of us unique and wonderful. We have gifts and talents and each has something to contribute. I recently won my first "Best Film" award. What might be the next achievement you reach?

* * * * *

My story is unique to me, and I don't know yet what the ending will look like. Everyone's outcome is different, but people on all locations of the autism spectrum deserve to have *their* best outcome. We all have things that are important to us, whether we can verbalize them or not.

We all have a purpose. We all need love, acceptance, and happiness. We also need to give love and acceptance to others. We need people who are in our corner and will fight alongside us, and we fight for them.

I also want people with autism to learn not to limit themselves because of their diagnosis. Just because socializing or sensory issues are overwhelming and challenging doesn't mean you should hide at home. Family members and friends of people with autism should try not to assume we can't handle certain situations or expectations. Give it a try, you may be surprised. It's going to be hard at first, but if it's something you really want it is worth taking those first steps.

You are important.

You belong in this world, so get out there and live your full life!

"Finally Home"

5 years old, dirt under my nails,
Throwing rocks at the bullies saying, "You're not a girl!"
Scared of my own shadow
I was in my own world.
Longing to be free from the trap in my mind,
Where the black hole of circles distorted the time.

But I fought with a champion's heart,
determined to shine.

Days burn.
Years pass.
They say it gets worse before better.
Found my own path.

I wish I had seen this letter:

You will be strong.
You will be loved.
You will be a person
whose people are loyal and true.

Don't be scared, love!
Don't hide your face, in your hands.
Look to the sun
it's where you belong
Keep moving on.

Learn more and follow Jennifer's story:

YouTube (Vlog) https://www.youtube.com/c/jennifermsumba

YouTube (Jen Msumba Music) https://www.youtube.com/user/TheGiz24

Stream/Download Music: https://ffm.to/jennifermsumba

Website: https://www.jennifermsumba.com/

Instagram: @jennifermsumba

TikTok: @jennifermsumba